The World as I See It

by Giulio Zambon

Copyright © Giulio Zambon, 2025

Giulio Zambon asserts the right to be identified as the author of this work.

All rights reserved. No part of this publication may be reproduced or transmitted in any form or by any means, electronic or mechanical, including photocopying, recording, or by any information storage or retrieval system, without prior written permission of the copyright owner.

This book is sold subject to the condition that it shall not, by way of trade or otherwise, be lent, resold, hired out or otherwise circulated without the copyright holder's prior consent in any form of binding or cover other than that in which it is published and without a similar condition including this condition being imposed on the subsequent purchaser.

ISBN: 978-0-6451827-2-9

Contents

....1

Preface..V

ME, SOCIETY, AND ETHICS......................................1

    Political Correctness..3

    Not Eating Animals, or Why I Am Vegetarian...........6

    I am an Apostate..10

    Remembering Patrizio Galli......................................16

    Banks!..20

    Dismissive People, Power, and all that....................22

    Speeding..28

    That's the Deal!...30

    Faster...31

    An Ethical Life..34

    A World of Exibitionists and Voyeurs.....................42

SCIENCE AND RESEARCH..44

    I.Q..46

    Science, the Scientific Method, and Hard Science Fiction..52

    Misunderstood Science: A question of probability...58

    Creativity and Research..62

The World as I see it

Reflections on Faith and Science 66

READING AND WRITING 72

Copyright, Copyleft, and Copywrong 74

Category Romance Novels 80

More than One Way of Reading 88

The Book Lives On 92

HISTORY 96

The Path to Terrorism 98

Prohibition 104

The Manifesto of Fascist Racism 110

Living in Italy during the Years of Lead 116

End-of-Year Cleanup 120

Soldiers and Dismembered Bodies. What else is New? 124

POLITICS 126

Marriage for All 128

Casualties 132

Checks on Senior Law-Enforcement Agents 134

Multiculturalism and Religion 138

Boat People 144

Drug Scores 150

Aboriginality 154

- Kill, Kill, Kill!..158
- John Kerry's Negationism.................................160
- Legalise them All...162
- Enough is Enough!...166

RELIGION..170
- Religion and Child Molestation.........................172
- The Ten Commandments..................................176
- A ban on Full Veils?...180
- The Responsibility of the Pope.........................184
- Is This True about Islam?.................................185
- The Catholic Church and Its Miracles...............188
- It's a Matter of Faith..192
- Faith and Buddhism...196

ARTIFICIAL INTELLIGENCE AND POSTHUMANISM..200
- The Future of Being Human.............................202
- Machines that Can Think.................................206
- Of Soft Brains and Software Brains..................216
- AI Doesn't Really Think...................................224
- From chipped stones to wearable computers..........228
- Technology that gets under your skin..............236

MANAGEMENT..242

- Management - Trust..243
- Management - Decisions..246
- Management - Where the Buck Stops....................248
- Management - Need to Know.................................250
- Management - Guidelines vs Rules........................252
- Management - Generosity.......................................256
- Management - My Leadership Principles...............258
- Appendix..262

Preface

In July 2010 I started writing a blog titled "Resistance is Futile", which I mainly used as a virtual soap box to express my opinions on ethics, science, society, religion, and politics.

In May 2021, after reviewing all the articles I had published, I decided to collect the most significant of them into the book of essays you are holding. Basically, *I liked what I had written!* There. I've said it.

But I didn't try to get it published and didn't publish it myself. Now it is the second half of 2025 and I am reviewing it once more.

I was surprised to discover that I found the ideas expressed in the articles still valid today, up to one and a half decades later.

Looking for an appropriated title, I stumbled on Albert Einstein's book *Mein Wetbild* (which literally translates to *My Worldview*) and decided to adopt the title that was given to its English translation.

I tried to group the essays in meaningful categories, although it wasn't easy because several articles could fit equally well in different categories.

I made some updates in some of the articles (and some further changes in this latest version), but they are minor and with negligible effects on the meaning of what I wrote then.

What follows is an outline of this book.

ME, SOCIETY, AND ETHICS

This section includes all articles that didn't fit neatly enough under the other headings. But I formed with these articles the first section precisely because they are more general in scope.

SCIENCE AND RESEARCH

You have to understand Science as a broad category that, for example, also includes Statistics. Perhaps because Statistics often is nothing else that using scientific methods to deceive people with numbers!

READING AND WRITING

This section only refers to individual books tangentially. It is more about how one reads and writes.

HISTORY

I initially had a single section to include both History and Politics. Perhaps it made sense, as the two subjects often overlap in my essays. In fact, also Society and Ethics always play a role. But I wanted to give you a better idea of what the main emphasis of each article was.

POLITICS

This is about political issues and decisions, mostly but not exclusively Australian.

RELIGION

The Catholic Church and Catholicisms are recurring themes in my essays. Perhaps it is because I was born and grew up in Rome, where one strongly feels the influence of the Vatican and is surrounded by hundreds of churches and thousands of clerics.

Also Islam appears in this section. I had considered keeping it separate from Catholicism, but it made more sense to me to keep them together.

AI AND POSTHUMANISM

It includes a series of essays I initially intended to use in a book titled Homo Novus (*Novus* is Latin for *New*).

MANAGEMENT

My main reason for writing about management is that I have a vision of a working society in which people are respected as human beings. I hate to see mature and intelligent adults conditioned and blackmailed into subservient roles by arrogant and careless bosses. I have to do something about it, even if it is just writing what few people will ever read.

Let's face it, despite all the talking about people being the biggest asset of a company, not enough managers really believe it, especially among those sitting on executive chairs. Bullies and sociopaths still have better chances of making career than those who prefer to work with people and avoid ruthelessly exploiting them. I know it from personal experience.

I believe that being hard-nosed is not necessary. It is possible to be firm without repressing, to be in control without handcuffing, and to tell without offending.

If you get from this book even a single new idea, it will have been worth publishing it. Let me know. You can reach me by writing to giulio@zambon.com.au

Canberra, 2025-10-01

The World as I see it

ME, SOCIETY, AND ETHICS

The World as I see it

Political Correctness

Political correctness has gone too far.

I can understand that women resent being excluded by collective terms like mankind and chairman. It makes sense to use humankind and chairperson instead, but to be gender-neutral with the pronouns creates difficulties. All these *he or she* and *his or her* are distractive, and the use of *they* and *them* when referring to a single individual makes me almost shiver in disgust. I usually use *[s]he* to replace *he/she*, but I have no alternative for *his/her*. The use of *hir* has not been universally accepted. Some non-fiction authors alternate between the masculine and the feminine pronouns, but it feels awkward. Sometimes I just use the feminine pronouns and leave it at that. After all, we have used the masculine ones for centuries, and it will take a long time before the men feel discriminated against.

But political correctness goes well beyond gender-neutrality.

The term *mentally retarded* has disappeared from the accepted vocabulary, together with the more detailed terms *idiot* (with an I.Q. sd 15 of 50-69), *imbecile* (20-49), and *moron* (below 20). Now we are supposed to say *mentally challenged* or *intellectually disabled* together with the qualifiers mildly, moderately, severely, and profoundly.

I suppose, I could still live with that. But in the past couple of years, the word *disabled* is also being banned. I believe that the current acceptable expression is *differently able*. But, to be blunt, I find that nonsensical: it is clear that a low IQ, blindness, or missing limbs make you *less* able to perform certain tasks. As long as we are respectful of the humanity inside a person, we should be able to speak more freely.

And what about replacing *short* or *dwarf* with *vertically challenged*, *garbage man* with *sanitation worker*, *homosexual man* with *gay*, *sex change* with *gender reassignment*, *handicapped* with p*hysically challenged*, or *differently abled*, *pornography* with *adult entertainment*, and *fat* with *full-figured*? And there are many more. Think for example at the growing list of terms to avoid excluding any sexually-related disposition: Lesbian, Gay, Bi-sexual, Transgender, Intersex, Queer. The list has become so long that we are forced to use the acronym LGBTIQplus.

Actually, I am a bit unhappy with the homosexuals' appropriation of the term *gay* because it prevents us from using it to indicate a moderately happy state, like in *The Gay Divorcee*, a 1934 film with Fred Astaire and Ginger Rogers. It is the lovely film in which Astaire's character, referring to the unexpected meeting with Ginger's character, says: "Chance is the fool's name for fate!"

Still talking about linguistic political correctness, in Australia we should also be careful not to say *aborigine* (noun) and *aboriginal* (adjective) when referring to native Australians. Some people might resent it.

Unfortunately, some groups use an expanded political correctness to boost their own agenda. For example, when disagreement with Israel's policies is stamped as antisemitism[1].

I was twice in Israel and felt no animosity whatsoever against its people. I spent a month in a kibbutz as a volunteer and then travelled throughout the country, from the Sea of Galilee to Eilat. In fact, it was in Degania Alef, the first kibbutz established in Israel in 1911, that I met the German young lady who later became my wife and with whom I still share my life. And Jerusalem is the most fascinating city I have ever seen. How could I possibly hate Israel and his people? I don't.

---

1 I made this point fifteen years ago, not expecting that it would become so important in today's political discourse.

And yet, I find Israel's handling of the Palestinians appalling[2], although my opposition to the Israeli policies has nothing to do with the Shoah and the centuries of prosecution of the Jews. In fact, I consider the fact that Israel identifies itself with Judaism an unacceptable, albeit for them very convenient, instrumentalisation of their national religion.

As an aside, I don't think that the Palestinian question will be resolved soon. Jerusalem is the third holiest city of Islam and, at the same time, the declared capital of Israel. The two parties will never agree to share it or partition it, unless they are forced to do so. And as long as the Jewish lobby in the U.S.A. remains as strong as it is today, the American governments will never force Israel to give up the full sovereignty on Jerusalem. I personally would like that Jerusalem were declared the religious equivalent of a world heritage site. A place where Jews, Muslims, and all sorts of Christians can have free access. A territory under U.N.O. administration not belonging to either a state of Palestine or to Israel. It would be an interesting precedent, wouldn't it?

Another aspect of our society associated with political correctness is the overwhelming and unjustified care with which one should talk about religion. Why shouldn't we be able to criticise religions as we criticise, say, political parties? I understand that people identify with their faith and take personal offence when criticism is made to their religion, but that is true for any deeply felt belief, isn't it? Everybody can verbally shoot at the atheist, but God forbid (pun intended) not at the faithful! Anyhow, I am slipping away from the subject of this article. Religion deserves an article of its own..

Originally posted in my blog on 2010-07-11.

---

[2] Again, I expressed this opinion in 2010. Nowadays, *criminal* would be more appropriate.

Not Eating Animals, or Why I Am Vegetarian

In this essay, I shall tell you how I became vegetarian. I expect that you will find it unreasonable and perhaps even a bit weird. In any case, regardless of of how you find it, I encourage you not to eat too much meat. It's not good for you.

I became vegetarian on January 1st, 1976. It was a new-year resolution. During the last hours of 1975, a medical doctor who also practised homoeopathy and acupuncture told me that animals being slaughtered respond to the stress of their violent death by generating in their tissues a series of toxins. He then argued that when we eat meat and fish we inevitably absorb those toxins, thereby damaging our physical and mental health. At the time, I found such a far-fetched theory convincing enough to make me say: "You know what? From tomorrow I will become vegetarian!" Don't ask me how I could even consider believing what in hindsight sounds like humbug. I have no idea. I had completely stopped drinking any type of alcoholic drink less than a couple of weeks before. Therefore, I cannot even claim that abundant libations to celebrate the coming of the new year had clouded my judgment. To my credit, I didn't believe in that theory for very long. That notwithstanding, my unwavering vegetarianism has accompanied me ever since.

I was obviously ready to become vegetarian, and even a dubious and unscientific theory was for me reason enough to take that step.

A story I had heard about wolves and feral dogs had certainly contributed to firming up my resolve. It's a nice story. The National Park of Abruzzo, smack in the middle of Italy, is the only place in the country where bears and wolves can be found in significant numbers. One of the park rangers told me that to protect the wolves they wanted to eliminate the many feral dogs that infested the park. The dogs competed with the wolves for food and, what was much worse, interbred with their wild cousins, thereby polluting their gene pool. The ranger told me that to get rid of the dogs, the only solution was to place everywhere poisoned baits. The wolves wouldn't touch them, while the feral dogs would eat them and die. "But," he said, "we have to keep doing it very assiduously because only dogs that have become feral recently eat the poisoned meat. After a few months in the wild, the dogs somehow re-learn the survival skills necessary for them to distinguish between what they can and cannot eat."

I found that story amazing (actually, inspiring). Despite generations and generations of selective breeding and life in captivity, in only a few months, the dogs were able to re-adapt to the wild. I asked myself: "Could we do it too? Could we 'civilised' humans re-discover the sensitivities that our ancestors must have certainly had? Perhaps, we can find within ourselves our ancient way of sensing what is good and what is bad for us."

I know: such a *genetic memory* might just be a myth. "Moreover," I thought, "if our conscious mind and the other higher functions of our brain mask the primitive instincts I am thinking about, how could one go about letting them emerge? Clearly, not by thinking about them. The only way must be an irrational one." I felt that being vegetarian was a step in the right direction. I felt that not eating animals would help me in my quest. It was a deep feeling, not based on any logical conclusion. I had to follow it.

You will now certainly be thinking something like: "Well, Giulio, did you achieve your goal? After decades of being vegetarian, have you rediscovered your ancient instincts? Can you detect when something would poison you?"

The brief answer is: "I don't know."

Considering that I tend to be overweight and that I struggle to get rid of my addiction to sugar, it would be reasonable to assume that I haven't achieved my goal. And yet, I still find the idea of ingesting parts of dead animals deeply disturbing. Perhaps it is just a fixation. Perhaps not. After all, Buddhist monks agree with me that one shouldn't eat that stuff. To explain the depth of my vegetarianism to some catholic friends, I once told them that for me eating the flesh of an animal was what they would call a mortal sin.

Originally posted in my blog on 2010-07-16.

The World as I see it

I am an Apostate

Yesterday (well, the day before I wrote this article), I stumbled onto a blog page[1] in which the author, a declared atheist, said (my translation from Italian): "Is there anybody who can help me to get a serious excommunication, possibly signed by the Pope?" This motivated me to write this article because I did get an official letter of excommunication from the Catholic Church, albeit not from the Pope himself. Perhaps, others will be inspired by my action and try to do the same.

As you know, Italy is considered to be a country almost completely Catholic. But this opinion is largely based on the fact that most people are baptised a few days after being born. My parents were not observant at all. I don't recall to have ever seen my mother go to church, and my father only went once a year on Palm Sunday to get a branch of olive tree. And yet, they baptised me at once. It had probably to do with the fact that it was a cultural tradition and that our relatives expected it. Or perhaps it was a leftover from the conditioning of the Fascist era.

In any case, the problem is that, once baptised, you are counted as a Catholic, even if you openly profess being an atheist, an agnostic, or belonging to another religion. This is because each diocese keeps a list of people who have been baptised and, once in, a name cannot be removed. But it is possible to have an annotation written beside your name to affirm the you no longer belong to the Roman Catholic Church. The process of requesting the writing of the annotation is called in Italian *sbattezzo*, which translates to *unchristening*.

---

[1] A page that, unfortunately, no longer exists:
danein.blog.kataweb.it/2009/07/31/scomuniche/

In Italy, Article 7 of the Legislative Decree No. 196 of 2003 states that the dioceses cannot refuse to make the annotation when somebody applies for it, and that they must confirm it to the applicant in writing. They don't make it easy for you though because you have to address your request directly to the parish where you were baptised.

I knew the name of my parish and, as it happened, I discovered that it had an email address. Normally, one is supposed to apply in writing, but on November 3rd, 2009, I sent the following email, based on an official template. My traslation into English tries to be as close as possible to the original, even if the clarity and perhaps the grammar will suffer. You will find the original email in Italian in the Appendix.

Subject: Request under article 7 of the Legislative Decree No. 196/2003.

From: Giulio Zambon

Date: Tue, 03 Nov 2009 15:13:29 +1100

To: sangiuseppe-crl@libero.it

To the Parson of the Parish St. Joseph at Via Nomentana

Via Francesco Redi 1

00161 Roma

I, the undersigned Giulio Zambon, born in Rome on [birth date removed], resident in Harrison (Australia) and registered in the register of the Italian citizens resident abroad (AIRE) of Rome, with the present request, presented under article 7, point 3, of the Legislative Decree No. 196/2003, I call on you as responsible for the Parish registry.

Having been Christened in your Parish, on a date that I don't know but closely subsequent to my birth, I wish that the datum in your possession be rectified, through annotation on the register of baptised, recognising my unequivocal will to be no longer considered a follower of the religious denomination "Roman Catholic Apostolic Church".

I further request to receive confirmation of the occurred annotation both via e-mail and via mail, duly undersigned and addressed to Giulio Zambon

[my sister's address in Italy removed]

Note that, in case of absent or inappropriate response to this request within 15 days, under article 145 of the Legislative Decree No. 196/2003, I reserve [the right] to refer [the matter] to the judicial authority or to file an appeal to the Guarantor for the protection of personal data.

I declare to immediately renounce any pause for reflection or afterthought regarding the above request; I warn [you] that I will consider any delay as a refusal to conform to the terms of the law (15 days according to article 146, point 2, of the legislative decree No. 196/2003) and that I will therefore resort to the judicial authority or to the Guarantor for the protection of personal data if you will illegally delay the requested annotation to a moment subsequent to the fifteenth day from receiving this request.

All this in agreement with the Legislative Decree No. 196/2003 (which has replaced the preceding Law No. 675/1996 from 1/1/2004), following the pronouncement of the Guarantor for the protection of personal data of 13/9/1999 and the sentence of the Court of Padua filed on 29/5/2000.

I warn you not to communicate the content of this request to third parties that are estraneous to the proceedings, and advise you that the distribution or communication to third parties of sensitive data can represent a violation of the Penal Code under article 167 of the Legislative Decree No. 196 of 2003.

I enclose photocopy of my passport to prove my identity.

Sincerely, Giulio Zambon

For the benefit of the Italian readers, you can download a model letter in RTF format from the website of the Italian Union of Atheist and Rationalist Agnostics (Unione degli Atei e degli Agnostici Razionalisti, www.uaar.it), where you will also find a full description of the *sbattezzo*.

As these applications must normally be sent via registered mail with acknowledgment of receipt, I didn't entirely expect to receive a reply. But I was pleasantly surprised by the efficiency of the diocese when a few weeks later I found in my letterbox the letter you will find at the end of this article.

It is a notarised copy of the letter sent by the diocese to my parish authorising the parson to write on the margin of my christening act that I no longer want to belong to the Catholic Church. It states that, as a result of my request, I can no longer act as a godfather in ceremonies of christening and confirmation, I will need an authorisation if I want to marry in the church, I am excluded from catholic funeral rites unless I show signs of repentance, I cannot take sacraments, and that I have been excommunicated l*atae sententiae* (passed sentence).

I believe that a similar procedure is also possible in Belgium and France, and that in Germany and Switzerland the religion is recorded by the state.

The World as I see it

VICARIATO DI ROMA

Roma, 11 novembre 2009

Oggetto: annotazione sul registro dei battezzati della volontà di non far più parte della Chiesa cattolica.

In riferimento all'istanza di ZAMBON GIULIO del giorno 3 novembre 2009, con la quale si chiede di non essere più considerato membro della Chiesa cattolica, si decreta quanto segue:

PREMESSO CHE
- per la Chiesa cattolica il Sacramento del battesimo conferisce uno *status* personale indelebile;
- la relativa annotazione negli appositi registri documenta un fatto storico, che come tale non può essere cancellato;
- la Chiesa cattolica, ordinamento giuridico indipendente e autonomo nel proprio ordine, ha il diritto nativo e proprio di acquisire, conservare e utilizzare per i suoi fini istituzionali i dati relativi alle persone dei fedeli, agli enti ecclesiastici e alle aggregazioni ecclesiali;

CONSIDERATO CHE

Le premesse sinteticamente richiamate hanno trovato conferma anche in pronunce del Garante per la protezione dei dati personali nelle quali è chiaramente riaffermato il pieno diritto della Chiesa cattolica alla tenuta dei registri dei battezzati, in piena ottemperanza alla legge n. 675/1996;

VISTO

L'art. 2, § 7 del Decreto Generale della Conferenza Episcopale Italiana del 30 ottobre 1999 recante "Disposizioni per la tutela del diritto alla buona fama e alla riservatezza",

SI AUTORIZZA

il Parroco della Parrocchia di San Giuseppe a Via Nomentana ad apporre a margine dell'atto di battesimo di Zambon Giulio (15/01/1950), ai sensi e per gli effetti della vigente normativa canonica, la seguente annotazione: "In forza del decreto dell'Ordinario diocesano, in data 11 novembre 2009 (Prot. N. 355/09), si annota che Zambon Giulio ha manifestato la volontà di non far più parte della Chiesa cattolica" (data dell'annotazione e firma del parroco).

Si fa presente che l'annotazione di cui sopra comporta per l'interessato le seguenti conseguenze di ordine canonico:
- esclusione dall'incarico di padrino per battesimo e confermazione (cfr. cann. 874, §1 e 893, §1);
- necessità della licenza dell'Ordinario del luogo per l'ammissione al matrimonio canonico (cfr. can. 1071, § 1, 4°);
- privazione delle esequie ecclesiastiche in mancanza di segni di pentimento (cfr. can. 1184, § 1,1°);
- esclusione dai sacramenti (cfr. cann. 1331, § 1, 2° e 915);
- scomunica latae sententiae (cfr. can. 1364,1).

L'Ordinario Diocesano

Originally posted in my blog on 2010-10-25.

The World as I see it

The World as I see it
Remembering Patrizio Galli

Only yesterday I discovered that Patrizio died almost one year ago, on August 20, 2010. I had lost contact with him some years ago and, until yesterday, my Internet searches had found nothing about him.

He was a colleague and a friend. The picture was taken in the Summer of 1983, on the Via Appia Antica, near Rome. I know, it's a bit old, but it is the only one I have of him. He is the one sitting on the column. The nice lady standing beside me is Monika, who was going to become my wife the following year, after we migrated to Australia.

He was a larrikin with an unstoppable sense of humour and an irreverent view on everything. I like to remember him as he appears on this picture, with a smile on his face.

The World as I see it

But last August a side of him emerged that would have better remained buried in the deepest recesses of his mind. In the hallway of his two-storey house near Rome, while his two teenage boys were sleeping upstairs, he armed his Smith & Wesson .44 Magnum revolver and shot five times his wife of twenty-six years, Catia. He then directed the gun towards himself and put an end to his own life. He was sixty-two. Catia was forty-seven.

It was the children, awoken by the gun shots, who discovered them. They immediately called for help, but it was too late. I cannot begin to imagine how they felt and how they could inform their three older sisters.

That morning, like many other times in the recent past, a heated argument had exploded between Catia and Patrizio. They were separating. Perhaps some financial difficulties didn't help, but I can only speculate on the reasons for the conflicts that ultimately led to such a tragedy.

Before Patrizio met Catia, he had had many fleeting relationships and seemed destined to remain an eternal bachelor. But Catia changed him. He became a devoted husband and a patient father, who never laid a hand on any member of his family.

He couldn't face the prospect of losing the love of his life. But how could he possibly do what he did, knowing that his children would have to live with this tragedy for the rest of their lives? Ultimately, every homicide/suicide is an act of selfishness and an affirmation of power. And yet, I only feel sadness and pain. I cannot bring myself to hate him for what he did. I feel as if he had been hit by a sudden sickness that in a second wiped out his rational mind.

The last time I saw him was in 2003. He showed me his collection of weapons, including the S&W. I still cannot grasp the fact that I held in my hand the weapon that a few years later would be used to kill. It was the revolver made famous by Clint Eastwood in the "Dirty Harry" movies. When it was built, it was claimed to be the most powerful hand gun in existence, and it was a monster. I have fired a .38 and a nine-millimetre, but they felt like toys compared to that .44 Magnum.

Besides being a fun person to be with, Patrizio was also one of the two or three best computer programmers I have ever met. Writing programs is like authoring prose: some people come up with lines that need little editing, sharp and clean. Patrizio was one of those. He was also one of the very few people I have ever met capable of reading a computer manual from cover to cover. And he was a natural, as he had never had any formal training in computer science.

This story of Patrizio is affecting me more than I would have thought.

I knew four people who committed suicide, and two of them quite well, and in two other occasions, I discovered somebody who had attempted to commit suicide. Also, a very close friend of mine died in a car accident when she was barely thirty years old. Therefore, it is not new for me to have to accept the violent death of somebody I know. And yet, this time it is different.

Somehow, I can understand suiciders. People don't fall into depression in a fraction of a second. In a sense, you prepare yourself to the eventuality that one day they might try it seriously enough to succeed, despite the best efforts of everyone who cares about them.

And car accidents, unfortunately, are a possibility that is always present in the back of our minds. At least, they are in mine.

But a murder is something else. I know that it did happen, but I still cannot imagine the Patrizio I know raising a monster of a gun and kill the love of his life. And he had to load it first. And then he fired at her five times, when I am sure that a single shot would have been enough. He just left in the drum a single bullet, to terminate his own life without having to reload.

This throws my perception of humanity into disarray. I had seen on TV similar cases, but I had thought that, somehow, I could have not had anything in common with those perpretators. I implicitly believed that I could have not possibly befriended them.

Then Patrizio.

Does it mean that everybody can do what he did? Almost certainly not. Could I do what he did? I don't think so. And yet perhaps everybody, pushed strongly enough, can do unimaginable things. It is a disturbing thought. I hope and trust that one day I will be able to shake it off, but not yet.

Death is always shocking, but these deaths will accompany me for a while. I don't believe in an afterlife, but I still feel compelled to say: Farewell my friend. Suffering is over.

Originally posted in my blog in two parts on 2011-08-06 and 2011-08-08.

Banks!

This morning, I saw an interesting advertisement in the window of a bank. It offered a yearly interest rate of 5.6% for a three-month term deposit (yes. In Australia we have high interest rates. This is one of the reasons why people pump up the value of the AUD by investing in it). Then, on the same ad, with the figures well aligned, it offered to pay 5.10% for a six-month term deposit.

Do you get it?

3 months: 5.6%
6 months: 5.10%

They expect the interest rates to decrease. Therefore, they offer a lower interest rate for six months than for three months. But, by writing 5.10 instead of 5.1, they make it look as if the interest rate for six months were higher than that for three months. They play on the ignorance of people who see 10 greater than 6 even if it is after a decimal period.

I hate banks... Almost as much as insurances...

Originally posted in my blog on 2012-02-05.

The World as I see it

Dismissive People, Power, and all that

Why do we dismiss somebody's opinion instead of considering what they have to say?

Imagine the situation: a dozen people are discussing around a table. Some never say anything (the "listeners"), while others speak, either on their own initiative or reacting to someone else's opinions (the "speakers").

Let's concentrate on how the speakers react to what other speakers say. A couple of them behave very differently depending on who's speaking. In some cases, they listen attentively, even taking notes, and respond with pertinent comments. In other cases, they start reading something, shake their heads, look towards the ceiling, or say something to one of their neighbours; then, often after a few seconds, they interrupt the speaker with something that has nothing to do with what was being said.

Does it sound familiar? It probably does because those know-it-all, closed-minded, and disrespectful people are everywhere. I have observed them all my life.

For me, when dealing with other people (actually, when dealing with anything at all!), respect is fundamental. I base all my relationships on respecting and being respected. One of my core beliefs is that, no matter how better in some ways I think I might be, nothing gives me the right to dismiss or even humiliate other human beings.

Are these "dismissers" unaware of being offensive or are they aware of it but don't care? And why do they do it?

Over the years, I have noticed that some of the dismissers (although not all) are courtesans. That is, followers. They like to rub shoulders with people in power, and tend to hop around their "masters" wagging their tails, like little dogs hoping for a pat on the back or a scrap of food. It's very unfortunate that their brown-nosing often lifts them to positions of responsibility or influence. When this happens, they tend to be very abrupt with their subordinates, while expecting from them unconditional love. With their behaviour, they perpetuate a culture of dismissiveness and disrespect.

This train of thought leads me to considering what power rests on. A lot has been written about the bases of power since 1959, when French and Raven published their study titled "The bases of social power". There are now several theories along those lines that involve a variable number of factors. A widely accepted theory is based on the following seven types of power:

- Coercive power: ability to mete out punishment.

- Reward power: ability to bestow rewards.

- Legitimate power: obtained as part of the position or job one holds.

- Referent power: due to being liked and respected.

- Connection power: ability to influence powerful people.

- Expert power: due to the abilities and skills one possesses.

- Informational power: due to having access to valuable or important information.

I am a bit at a loss in identifying somebody whose coercive and reward powers do not come as a result of some other type of power. In organisations and also in society in general, coercive and reward powers are part of legitimate power. Somebody you love can reward or punish you without any legitimate power, but isn't it because [s]he already has referent power over you?

For a different reason, I also don't feel entirely comfortable with the concept of referent power. I agree that when you are liked and respected by people, you have power over them. But how did you gain that appreciation? This type of power seems to originate, at least to a large extent, from other powers. If somebody dismisses me from the very start because I am in no position of power, don't know powerful people, and is not immediately apparent what I know and can do, how can I possibly gain his/her respect?

There are some people that you cannot help liking from the moment you meet them, either because they are beautiful and sexy, because of their penetrating gaze, or because of some other physical features they possess. Some politicians and actors have this "presence" that makes them the centre of attention. This seems a subset of referent power, but I would classify it separately, perhaps with the term "charisma", to distinguish it from the referent power that is acquired over time.

In most cases, whether you are or not dismissed from the very start depends on your position (direct or by connection) or charisma (or both). Unless people have had the opportunity to learn about you beforehand, they will not recognise in you an expert and/or a holder of worthwhile information.

Charisma is purely irrational. It's mojo. Magic. Sometimes, people call it "natural leadership", but it has nothing to do with being able to make good decisions on the basis of limited information and then follow them up by motivating people into action. Although, perhaps, without a dose of charisma, you can manage people but cannot really lead them. I'm not concerned about charisma because being charmed by charismatic people doesn't make people dismissive of others.

The dismissive people are those who are really only interested in what's good for them. They don't care about your feelings or anybody else's. That's why they only listen to the boss, those who can influence the boss, and people who can tell them something they might use. Everybody else is a nuisance. Nothing more than a distraction. They have no patience for them.

These people don't see others as treasure chests of feelings, life experiences, emotions, and ideas. In charities and other volunteer-based organisations, they often are the zealots who like to be in the "inner circle" and use efficiency as an excuse for ignoring you.

So far, I have described a somewhat extreme case of dismissers, but, unfortunately, the world is full of mild dismissers. That is, narrow-minded people who haven't managed to see beyond the confines of their parochial upbringings; myopic people who perceive novelty and difference as threats rather than opportunities to broaden their minds.

Indeed, very many tend to ignore, avoid, reject, or even despise those who appear to be different from them. It does make sense to link up with people with whom you share experiences, opinions, or tastes. But I found that the vast majority of people become defensive when they discover that you have made important life choices different from theirs. It is as if your existence were enough to undermine the raison d'être of their whole life.

Perhaps I am digressing, but what I'm trying to say in my contorted way is that, ultimately, the dismissiveness I have been talking about is nothing else than selfishness combined with a very common form of obtuseness.

I have a further reflection concerning expert and informational powers.

When applying for jobs during my IT and management career, I was almost always been asked to provide proof of knowledge and experience related to the job I was applying for. Obviously, why should a company hire somebody who needs training, rather than somebody else who already knows what it's all about?

And yet, there is another factor that is almost invariably dismissed: how quickly can the new hire learn? How long will it take for him/her to become more productive than somebody who has previous knowledge of the matter but is inflexible and slow in learning?

Once, after migrating to Germany, I applied for a job with Messerschmitt-Bölkow-Blohm in Hamburg. I had only studied German, ab initio, for four months. And yet, the entire interview with MBB was conducted in German. I didn't get the job because they wanted to have somebody with a better knowledge of German. How stupid was that? If I could be interviewed in German after a few months, how long would it have taken me to progress to the point where my language would no longer be a problem? Indeed, I then got a job with AEG-Telefunken and quickly became a productive member of the group.

An endemic problem of our society is the failure to distinguish between knowledge and intellectual capabilities. When talking about a computer, very few would confuse microprocessor speed with memory or disk drive capacity. But when it comes to human minds, the amount of information that one has been able to cram into his brain is often considered proof of intelligence.

We can discuss the validity of IQ tests to measure intelligence, but one thing is clear: the higher the IQ, the more a person can perceive complex patterns, analyse problems, and extract logical information because that's what IQ tests measure. It means that high-IQ people can more easily acquire technical and scientific knowledge, where the main difficulty is in understanding rather than remembering.

Then, why is IQ a taboo subject? Is it because people are afraid that theirs is too low? Is it a mind-equivalent of most males' fear of having too small a penis?

Originally posted in my blog on 2012-06-04.

Speeding

In Australia, like in many western countries, we have speed cameras.

What is odd, though, is that their position is announced in advance with big street signs (at least in the Australian Capital Territory, where I live). Speed cameras are called here "speed traps". But what trap is visibly marked so that the prey doesn't "fall" into it?

There are some mobile cameras, but very few. Often, instead of being used by the police to issue speeding tickets, they are connected to big panels that tell you your speed, as if the speedometer mounted in your dashboard were not enough.

Canberrans are up in arms whenever the government announces more speed cameras. In the newspapers, you read articles accusing the Police of being money grabbers. It is as if the Police didn't have the right to fine you when you break the law. Evidently, the motorists think they have the right to exceed the speed limits.

I say, fill the territory with speed cameras and place police cars with Doppler radars around curves, at the bottom of down slopes, and hidden in the shrubs! Hit as many speeders as possible and hit them hard for breaking the law in a way that endangers everyone. Indeed, most accidents occur because people drink & drive and/or speed. Breath checks are good, but they also slow down the traffic. Speed checks don't.

The Swiss do it right: Zurich has dozens of speed cameras, which take very precise measurements of car speeds (how could it be otherwise? They are Swiss! :-). But fines are only issued if the measured speed exceeds the speed limit by more than 5 km/h. By giving a margin of 5 km/h, they generously take into account tolerances. I was once fined forty Swiss Francs (about $40 at the time) because my speed was 6 km/h above the speed limit. Fair enough.

Let the speeders be annoyed that they get caught. I don't know how much the fines are because I have never been fined since I came back to Australia in 2008[1], but I say: make them higher. Sooner or later, people will start thinking that speeding doesn't pay.

Originally posted in my blog on 2012-08-01.

---

1 Actually, a few years ago I got a fine of more than $100 accompanied by two demerit points for driving at 60 km/h in a 40 km/h zone. I had not seen the sign, but that is no excuse...

The World as I see it

That's the Deal!

Some time ago, at the cafeteria of the University of Canberra, I ordered a muffin and a short black coffee and was asked to pay five dollars.

Yesterday, I went again to the same cafeteria, again ordered a muffin and a short black and was told to pay $6.70. When I picked up the coffee from the lady who was working the espresso machine, I asked: "When is the offer of $5 for a coffee and a muffin valid?"

"Why, always." She answered.

"Then why was I asked to pay $6.70? I want my 1.70 back!" I said while smiling.

At that point, the lady who had been at the cash register came back and told me that the special offer of $5 for a sweet and a coffee was for a medium-sized coffee, not for a short one.

I pointed out that clearly the offer was designed to exclude large coffees, which cost more, not small black ones, which use less energy, less coffee, less water, and no milk.

I found it so outrageous that I couldn't let her get away with such nonsense. Finally, after some insistence from my part, she relented and refunded me my $1.70. But she was clearly annoyed and, while giving me the money, she complained "But that's the deal..."

Originally posted in my blog on 2013-01-18.

Faster

I just read the book *Faster - The Acceleration of Just About Everything*, by James Gleick, the well-known author of *Chaos*. I picked up a copy of the book in a reminders' bookshop and it was a very good buy.

Gleick analyses the roots of the frenetic and ever faster modern life. The book was first published fifteen years ago, but it hasn't aged at all. What follows is my interpretation of the essence of the book and my reflections on its content.

The world has become very competitive. As a result, everybody keeps looking for "an edge". That is, for something that will give them a bit of an advantage over their competitors. This applies to every organisation and individual living in a modern society, and especially in western-style capitalistic societies.

An edge could consist of working a little bit longer, employing a new technique or tool, optimising our time, exploiting other people's work, focussing on what counts most, and, effectively, anything that will increase our output, either in terms of quality or (more often) in terms of quantity.

How we use/spend/employ/waste/enjoy our time, according to Gleick (and I agree), is of paramount importance. That's why we keep looking at our watch; that's why we are so impatient; that's why we hate queues; that's why we plan and prioritise our days.

Unfortunately, every edge we develop has already been developed by others, or soon will be. In our attempt to emerge from the masses and be successful, we keep struggling up a downward escalator, whereby failure to become more productive means going backward. And, to push the metaphor further, the downward escalator doesn't move at uniform speed. It accelerates.

The World as I see it

This is an intrinsically unstable system, in which a positive feedback leads to explosive conclusions: we work harder and faster to emerge but, as everybody else does it as well, we need to work even faster. This has made possible incredible achievements, but we are paying those achievements with our health and wellbeing.

It wasn't always like this. Before the industrial revolution or even just before the introduction of production lines, time was not money. But for the past good one hundred years everything is money, including time. Even if, unlike money and despite colloquialisms, time cannot be gained or saved: every second spent is lost forever and cannot ever been recovered.

H.G. Wells, in his "A Modern Utopia" of 1905, described a future in which we would work five hours a week. Modern technology might allow us to do so, but the increase in efficiency and productivity generated by technology, instead of automatically resulting in a reduction of working hours, is used to a large extent to fuel growth and enrich the financial elite. The average number of weekly working hours has been steadily falling in developed countries, but we are still very far from the Utopian levels predicted by Wells.

During my working life in Italy, Germany, Australia, Switzerland, and France, I was steadily under pressure to work longer hours. Australia was the worst offender, and I often had to work 60 h/week or more. You might think that it was because I was slow or not good enough, but that was not the case. Everybody around me struggled. When I worked at Prime R&D in Canberra, we had a HR person to take care of only thirty engineers. Such a very high ratio (1/30) was deemed necessary to enable us to survive the pressure we had to endure and the resulting conflicts. Indeed, the strain caused two engineers to faint.

Perhaps I enjoyed reading *Faster* because what he wrote resonated with what I had experienced.

The book is also full of snippets of time-related information that I found very interesting.

For example, at MacDonald's, *in 1997 its marketers tried to speed up [...] by offering refunds to any customer not served within fifty-five seconds* (p.245). That's what I would call a pressure-cooker environment, even if at MacDonald's everything is fried! ;-)

Originally posted in my blog on 2014-04-13.

An Ethical Life

I just finished reading *Writings on an Ethical Life*, by Peter Singer.

For those who don't know him, Peter Singer is a philosopher who has become very controversial because of some of his positions, which he expressed without compromising clarity in order to adhere to political correctness. This book is in my opinion a must-read for everybody who is concerned with moral and ethical issues.

In an interview conducted by Bob Abernethy and shoved on WNET-TV on 20 September 1999, he expressed very clearly the key concepts that form the basis of his positions (a transcript of the interview is included in the book). In response to the very first question, he stated:

> *First, it is important to say that in my view [...] a human being doesn't have value simply in virtue of belonging to the species Homo Sapiens. Species membership alone isn't enough. The qualities that I think are important are, first, a capacity to experience something—that is, a capacity to feel pain, or to have any kind of feelings. That's really basic. But then that's something we share with a huge range of nonhuman animals. In addition, when it comes to a question of taking life, or allowing life to end, I would say it matters whether a being is the kind of being who can see that he or she actually has a life—that is, can see that he or she is the same being who exists now, who existed in the past, and who will exist in the future.*
>
> *I use the term "person" to refer to a being with that kind of self-awareness—in the words of the philosopher James Rachels, a being who can live a biographical life and not merely a biological*

life. A person has a lot more to lose when his or her life is ended than a being that is conscious, and can feel pain, but nevertheless is conscious of its existence only moment by moment, experiencing only one moment of consciousness and then the next, without understanding the connection between them.

One of the results of his position is that in his opinion parents should be able to choose to kill their newborn child if it was born with conditions so severe that doctors don't really try to keep it alive. In Singer's words, "It would be justifiable to take active steps to end that infant's life swiftly and more humanely than by allowing death to come through dehydration, starvation, or an untreated infection".

Clearly, such positions have generated a lot of controversy. But I have to ask, once political correctness and absolute truths based on faith rather than logic are left behind, how can anybody disagree with such a statement? The sanctity of human life advocated by many (perhaps most) is based on the concept that human beings are made in the image of God and should be treated in a special way purely because they belong to the species Homo Sapiens. But a baby, as a being, is no different from other mammals. In fact, it can be argued that, given the choice between saving an adult chimpanzee and a human baby with spina bifida, we should save the chimpanzee. An adult chimpanzee has a past and looks forward to a future life, while a human infant has no past and is not self-aware.

In general, I find that too often society reacts to ideas and events because it is perceived that people have to react that way, rather than because they have thought the whole matter through. This is not the first time that I mention my hatred for political correctness (and empty politeness, although that's another matter).

The World as I see it

Nowadays, you cannot disagree with some policies of the state of Israel or condemn some acts of the Israeli army without being accused of anti-semitism. Well, I believe that Israel has no moral right to keep the people in Gaza captive and prevent ships from supplying them. Hamas shouldn't send rockets to Israel. It is, in fact, an activity that I found unacceptable and, frankly, also counterproductive. But the Israeli government really are bullies. And I am not for this an anti-semite!

You cannot observe that blacks and whites are different without being accused of being racist. If you search the Internet, you will find that for decades people have argued about differences of IQ between ethnic groups. Somebody wrote that blacks (or Africans? I don't remember) have on average a lower IQ than European and that Asians (or Chinese?) have an average IQ higher than Europeans. And so what? First of all, we are talking of measurements that are not as straightforward as measuring heights of weights. With these IQ tests, the only thing that you can be certain of is what the scores are. Certainly not what they mean and what they exactly measure. Secondly, there are so many factors that have an influence on the capacity to solve tests, ranging from education to nutrition, from health to how much coffee you have drunk before sitting for the test. Even if it were true that blacks have lower average scores, very many blacks will still score better than most Europeans and Chinese!

And then, of course there is sexism. Human females have smaller brains than males. That is a fact. Am I being sexist? Probably not, unless I were then to say that women are therefore less intelligent (whatever that means) than men. But I certainly don't believe so. And what if I were to say that women are on average more emotional than men? Perhaps such a statement has no basis in reality. But would I be sexist if I were to believe it (I don't actually have an opinion either way)? And can I allow myself to compliment the look of a woman without being accused of objectifying her simply because so many men and women are concerned with how one looks? Whoof...

Another concept that cannot be contradicted with impunity in modern society is that everybody is equal. Now, I believe that everybody should have the right to achieve the maximum level of fulfillment in their lives. But to say that everybody's needs and capabilities are the same is nonsense. *We are all different!* I know, this can become an excuse for accepting or causing injustice, but by denying that we are different from each other, we run other risks. For example, physically disabled people are different from people with fully-abled bodies. If we were to deny it, we couldn't possibly advocate the presence of ramps in buildings, could we? Peter Singer was accused of advocating euthanasia of disabled adults because of his position about unviable newborn babies. Come on!

In all cases, the key is respect. As long as I respect the people I am in contact with, regardless of their color, size, gender, beliefs, and sexual orientation, I must be able to say what I believe to be true. Or should I be denied to tell somebody that I think they are incompetent simply because he/she is black, or a woman, or gay, and my criticism might be interpreted as discrimination? Let's face it: a stupid, as well as a genius, can come in any colour and shape!

What follows is a short section (short enough not to violate copyright, I believe) of Peter Singer's book that resonates a lot with what I believe. The section title is *Toward an Ethical Life* and was first publishe in 1993 in the book *How Are We to Live?*

> *In a society in which the narrow pursuit of material self-interest is the norm, the shift to an ethical stance is*

more radical than many people realize. In comparison with the needs of people starving in Somalia, the desire to sample the wines of the leading French vineyards pales into insignificance. Judged against the suffering of immobilized rabbits having shampoos dripped into their eyes, a better shampoo becomes an unworthy goal. The preservation of old-growth forests should override our desire to use disposable paper towels. An ethical approach to life does not forbid having fun or enjoying food and wine, but it changes our sense of priorities. The effort and expense put into buying fashionable clothes, the endless search for more and more refined gastronomic pleasures, the astonishing additional expense that marks out the prestige car market from the market in cars for people who just want a reliable means of getting from A to B—all these become disproportionate to people who can shift perspective long enough to take themselves, at least for a time, out of the spotlight. If a higher ethical consciousness spreads, it will utterly change the society in which we live.

We cannot expect that this higher ethical consciousness will become universal. There will always be people who don't care for anyone or anything, not even for themselves. There will be others, more numerous and more calculating, who earn a living by taking advantage of others, especially the poor and the powerless. We cannot afford to wait for some coming glorious day when everyone will live in loving peace and harmony with everyone else. Human nature is not like that at present, and there is no sign of its changing sufficiently in the foreseeable future. Since reasoning alone proved incapable of fully resolving the clash between self-interest and ethics, it is unlikely that rational argument will persuade every rational person to act ethically. Even if reason had been able to take us further, we would still have had to face the reality of a world in which many people are very far from acting on the basis of reasoning of any kind, even crudely self-interested reasoning. So for a long time to come, the world is going to remain a tough place in which to live.

Nevertheless, we are part of this world and there is a desperate need to do something now about the conditions in which people live and die, and to avoid both social and ecological disaster. There is no time to focus our thoughts on the possibility of a distant utopian future. Too many humans and nonhuman animals are suffering now, the forests are going too quickly, population growth is still out of control, and if we do not bring greenhouse gas emissions down rapidly, the lives and homes of 46 million people are at risk in the Nile and Bengal delta regions alone. Nor can we wait for governments to bring about the change that is needed. It is not in the interests of politicians to challenge the fundamental assumptions of the society they have been elected to lead. If 10 percent of the population were to take a consciously ethical outlook on life and act accordingly, the resulting change would be more significant than any change of government. The division between an ethical and a selfish approach to life is far more fundamental than the difference between the policies of the political right and the political left.

We have to take the first step. We must reinstate the idea of living an ethical life as a realistic and viable alternative to the present dominance of materialist self-interest. If a critical mass of people with new priorities were to emerge, and if these people were seen to do well, in every sense of the term—if their cooperation with each other brings reciprocal benefits, if they find joy and fulfillment in their lives—then the ethical attitude will spread, and the conflict between ethics and self-interest will have been shown to be overcome, not by abstract reasoning alone, but by adopting the ethical life as a practical way of living and showing that it works, psychologically, socially, and ecologically.

Anyone can become part of the critical mass that offers us a chance of improving the world before it is too late. You can rethink your goals and question what you are doing with your life. If your present way of living does not stand up against an impartial standard of value, then you can change it. That might mean quitting your job, selling your house, and going to work for a voluntary organization in India. More often, the commitment to a more ethical way of living will be the first step of a gradual but far-reaching evolution in your lifestyle and in your thinking about your place in the world. You will take up new causes and find your goals shifting. If you get involved in your work, money and status will become less important. From your new perspective, the world will look different. One thing is certain: you will find plenty of worthwhile things to do. You will not be bored or lack fulfillment in your life. Most important of all, you will know that you have not lived and died for nothing, because you will have become part of the great tradition of those who have responded to the amount of pain and suffering in the universe by trying to make the world a better place.

Amen.

Originally posted in my blog on 2014-06-22.

The World as I see it

The World as I see it

A World of Exibitionists and Voyeurs

On 2014-07-25, the Los Angeles Times wrote: "Google reportedly finalizes deal for live stream service Twitch".

In case you don't know, Twitch Interactive offers live streaming of people playing video games.

Google paid 1G$ (1 billion US dollars) to gain control of Twitch. It sounds outragious to me, perhaps because I stopped playing widegames when PacMan and Pong were the rage of the time. But it makes sense: Twitch has 45 million unique viewers per month (up from 3.2M since the site was launched three years ago). "Twitchers" spend daily an average of 106 minutes watching somebody else play video games, and 58% of them do it for more than 20h a week. And when Google will merge Twitch into YouTube, you can reasonably expect that more live activities will be added.

OK. I admit it: all the craze of the past decade to post selfies and videos has never excited me. I don't have this urge to show myself to the world. What motivates me to publish this blog is the hope (dare I say *knowledge*?) that, among all the chaff I write, there is something that people will find useful. Buried among the articles about how to fold toilet paper or containing micro-fiction, there are more serious articles. My most-viewed top three articles explain programming techniques and have so far collected 11,484 page views[1]. Very far from the millions of hits of successful videos, but it still gives me a warm and fuzzy feeling to think that I helped thousands of people in a practical way.

Humans are social animals. We have to give credit to people like Mark Zuckerberg to have recognised it and to have been

---

[1] That was obviously years ago. I haven't bothered to update the number.

able to capitalise on it. It is, in a sense, the logical evolution of the tabloid magazines. A major difference though is that now everybody can feel a bit like a celebrity, especially if [s]he agrees to bare body and soul to the world!

FaceBook, Instagram, YouTube, Flicker, TikTok, and the rest of the "social" web sites let everyone give in to exibitionism and, at the receiving end, voyeurism. I don't understand how people can spend hours reading and writing gossip. I only like YouTube because it lets me see old TV programs in B&W and performances of my favourite singers.

The success of Twitch is just one more confirmation of this exibitionism/voyeurism compact that drives the Internet (besides porn, of course).

Originally posted in my blog on 2014-07-28.

SCIENCE AND RESEARCH

The World as I see it

I.Q.

I had known of the existence of Mensa for longer than four decades and had considered taking their admission test since my university years but, for one reason or another, I only did it last year[1]. As it happened, it was precisely on my sixtieth birthday. When I was told that it would take up to two months to know the result of the test, I explored the Web and discovered that there were many other High-IQ societies. And many of them had stricter criteria than Mensa. Now, Mensa at the time (at least in Australia) only said whether the candidates had an I.Q. within the top 2% of the population or not. In other words, they didn't actually tell you your I.Q. That's one of the reasons why I started answering some of the many I.Q. tests available online.

Wikipedia defines intelligence as follows: Intelligence is an umbrella term describing a property of the mind including related abilities, such as the capacities for abstract thought, understanding, communication, reasoning, learning, learning from past experiences, planning, and problem solving. Given such a broad definition, it is not surprising that there is not one simple way to measure intelligence. Somebody who is clever at solving word puzzles and playing Scrabble, is not necessarily as good in figuring out three-dimensional geometrical problems. Therefore, different tests measure different cognitive abilities. Moreover, the results of I.Q. tests depend on a series of other factors, like tiredness, emotional state, use of substances like alcohol and coffee, and others. Ultimately, an I.Q. test measures the ability to answer intellectually non-trivial questions of one or more types and under specific circumstances. If we group the people on the basis of how many questions they are able to answer in an I.Q. test and arbitrarily assign the value of I.Q. = 100 to the

---

1 That is, in 2009.

average, we obtain a normal distribution as shown in Figure 1 (freely downloadable from Wikipedia).

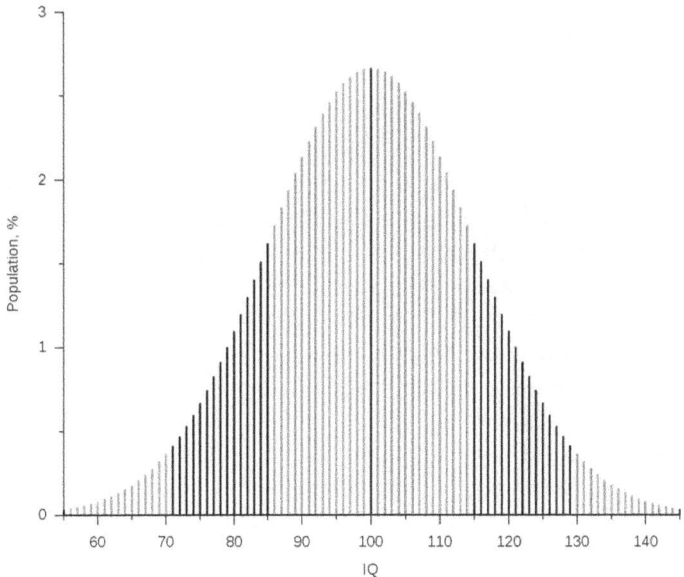

Figure 1: I.Q. curve

To define an I.Q. scale, besides choosing 100 to indicate the peak of the distribution, you also have to decide how finely you want to divide the range of possible values. This is done in Statistics by defining the size of the interval that comprises 68% of the whole population. In Figure 1, it corresponds to the darker grey bands adjacent to the peak (I know, it is not clearly visible). Half of that interval is called the standard deviation (or sd) of the distribution. As you can see, the sd was set to 15. As a result of this (entirely arbitrary) decision, 68% of the world population is said to have an I.Q. between 85 and 115. Unfortunately, different researchers have chosen different values of standard deviation. The two most widely used are 15 and 16, but I am told the standard deviation used in Italy is 24. Therefore, when you say what I.Q. you have, you also have to specify the standard deviation you are using. For example, the I.Q. you need to qualify for Mensa can be expressed as 131 sd15, 134 sd16, or 150 sd24, all corresponding to the top 2% scores of the population. Just providing an I.Q. without the sd it was measured with is meaningless.

I personally prefer to talk in terms of percentiles instead of IQs. For example, you qualify for Mensa if you are in the top 2%. This means that only 2% of the world population has an I.Q. as high or higher than yours. Isn't it much clearer than talking about I.Q. and standard deviations? If you then divide 1 by your percentile, you obtain what is known as the *rarity* of your intelligence. For example, a 2% means that walking in a crowded place, only one person out of 1/0.02 = 50 will be as intelligent as (or more intelligent than) you are. If you qualify for Mensa, when you go to a theatre with an audience of 500 people, you can assume that approximately 490 of them are less intelligent than you are.

When I finally got the results from Mensa, I was not surprised to have qualified because in the meanwhile I had passed several other tests (shown in the table overleaf).

Since I passed these tests, two of them (Titan and Get-Y) have been disqualified because somebody had posted some answers on the Web, thereby invalidating all the subsequent tests. It's a pity because they were very good tests, but some people cannot keep their mouth shut.

As you can see, there is quite a bit of variability. Against every logic, I like to think that my I.Q. is close to the maximum value I have achieved. It's heady to think that in the city where I live there are perhaps only 100 people as intelligent as (or more intelligent than) me![1]

---

1 Considering that Canberra has a population approaching 500,000.

The World as I see it

Test Name	I.Q. sd15	%	Rarity	Link
Mysterium	138	0.50	200	www.mysteriumsociety.org/exam4.html
Kvociento	145	0.13	741	elateneos.freehostia.com/kvociento.html
Titan	146	0.12	909	www.eskimo.com/~miyaguch/titan.html
Get-Y	144	0.18	556	No longer available
X-test	153	0.02	5000	www.box.net/shared/crmxm2afha
TEQUINMA	151	0.04	2709	epida.webs.com/TEQUINMA%20english.doc

I am currently member of nine High-IQ societies, with entry requirements ranging between 5% (I.Q. 124 sd15) and 0.06% (I.Q. 149 sd15), but there are people I know who are members of many more societies. The world of High-IQ societies is at times baffling. There is even a society that requires a rarity of 1,000 billions. Obviously, as there are about 7.8 billions people on Earth, such a society should hardly have even a single member. And yet, as surprising as it might be, the society does have a member. But it is thanks to a trick, as I will explai in a moment.

How would you like to be member of a very exclusive High-IQ society? I'll tell you the trick: make one. If you start a new High-IQ society, as the founder, nobody can prevent you from becoming a member of it, regardless of your actual I.Q.!

Another thing: If you check out the PARS society (https://www.iqsociety.org/societies/pars/), you will see that the it requires an I.Q. in the top 0.00003% (I.Q. 175 sd15). Now, it turns out that founders and directors of "recognised High I.Q. societies" can join as honorary members. That is, without ever having taken an I.Q. test, you can create a High-IQ society with an interesting enough declared purpose and the I.Q. requirement you fancy. Then, when you have managed to attract, say, 20 members, nothing prevents you from applying for membership to the PARS society, and there is no reason why they should reject you. After that, you will be able to exchange messages and participate in discussions with the "elite" of the High-IQ world. Baloney!

The main activity of most High-IQ societies consists of discussing issues of common interest in the society's forum. Sometimes the discussions go off the tangent with supposedly brilliant and amusing remarks. It is clear that one deals with people of above-average intelligence, but that doesn't always/necessarily make for interesting discussions[1].

Originally posted in my blog on 2010-08-14.

---

[1] That's why I have severed most contacts to the world of High-I.Q societies.

The World as I see it

Science, the Scientific Method, and Hard Science Fiction

Non-scientists find it difficult to comprehend that scientific theories cannot ever be completely proved. No theory is ever "final", but with the passing of time, as new experiments and refined measurements keep verifying it, a theory becomes the foundation upon which scientists can build new theories. As a scientist, you can believe in the validity of a theory and, provisionally, do as if it were completely certain, while knowing in the back of your mind that a new fact discovered tomorrow might not fit into it. When that happens, especially with well established theories, the obvious reaction is to find a way of extending the theory to include the new fact.

In a sense, a theory that has worked well in many cases cannot ever be disproved. You just need to know when it can be applied. For example, Newtonian Mechanics is perfectly correct in your everyday life. You don't need to be concerned with relativistic or quantum effects when catching a bus!

Consider the Theory of Evolution. The bigots (according to Wikipedia, a bigot is a person obstinately or intolerantly devoted to his or her own opinions and prejudices) who push for Intelligent Design to be taught in schools have no idea of what a scientific theory is, and have no qualms in proposing their beliefs as an alternative to Darwinian Evolution. They insist on the word "theory" associated with Evolution without realising that, by doing so, they only show their scientific ignorance. After so many decades, Darwinian Evolution has survived every criticism thrown at it, and every new discovery in Molecular Biology keeps confirming its validity. Therefore, even if tomorrow somebody discovered something that doesn't fit into it, it will not change the fact that the Theory of Evolution by Natural Selection applies to us, the dinosaurs, the amoebas, and the rest of species that populate earth.

The World as I see it

One problem is that many (perhaps most) people find it difficult to cope with uncertainty. They "need" to believe in something, to be certain that it is true. Dare I say that the less intelligent people are, the more they depend on certainties? It makes sense because it is easier to deal with simple choices than having to evaluate complex factors and cope with fuzzy ideas. Then, everything becomes black or white, without shades of grey; stereotypes drive your behaviour; and a priest, speaking on behalf of a God who is by definition unprovable, tells you what is right or wrong. How easy is that?

Another debate that only shows scientific ignorance is the one about climate change. Even the question "do you believe in it?" is nonsensical because it is not a matter of belief at all. Changes have been measured and the influence of humanity is clear. But even if it were not, it would still remain a stupid debate because, regardless of how much humanity contributes to them, climate changes are going to cause us problems soon.

We have been cutting forests, burning in decades what took millions of years to put into the ground, using up natural resources as if they were unlimited, and creating substances that don't exist in nature. You can bet your arse (*ass* for the American readers) that sooner or later you will have to pay the bill for all that. The only questions are when, how high the price, and in what currency. If the earth climate reaches a tipping point, like the stopping of the Gulf Stream, just to mention a possible one, we are going to regret to have wasted so much time debating whether computer models are credible or what influence the Sun spots have on our temperature.

The effects of science and technology have become pervasive in our modern world. Science is too important to be considered a subject of choice. We should teach the scientific method in all schools. Physics should become a compulsory subject, beside literature and languages. It would

The World as I see it

automatically resolve many of the senseless debates that afflict us today.

I wouldn't be surprised if the huge technological development in computing has had a deleterious effect on understanding science. The reason is that films and computer games show what is physically impossible as if it were real. Already the battering that Bruce Willies, Silvester Stallone, and Arnold Schwarzenegger could endure in their action movies of some years ago was superhuman. But today's Computer Generated Images (CGI) completely remove the boundaries between reality and fantasy. The children that grow up with these images think that everything is possible.

Many years ago, when Wile E. Coyote ran past the edge of the cliff and looked down suspended in mid air before falling, he was violating the laws of Physics. But he was clearly a cartoon character. It was funny to see him precisely because he and the Roadrunner were unrealistic.

Compared with the fantastic worlds we see on the screen today, our real world is unexciting. Some people respond to these stimuli by seeking the thrills of extreme sports. Many others just look for "more": more exciting, more entertaining, more extreme, more fantastic, ... It doesn't surprise me that Science Fiction has become a minor component of what has become to be known as Speculative Fiction.

SpecF is used to collectively indicate Fantasy, Horror, and SF, but you only need to go to a bookshop to see that the SpecF shelves are full of extremely thick books about dragons, elves, wizards, vampires, zombies, and people with supernatural powers.

Not much SF around these days, and even less of what I call "Hard Science Fiction" (HSF). That is, a work of fiction that relies for its existence on scientific or technological facts.

The World as I see it

When Jules Verne in 1865 wrote "De la Terre à la Lune" (From the Earth to the Moon), he got it wrong: you cannot use a mass of expanding gas to propel a payload into space as, in any case, the initial acceleration would kill you. But Verne gave birth to the idea of reaching into space with technological means rather than, say, being transported on the wings of an angel.

It is not necessary for a HSF story to be consistent with all scientific knowledge we currently have. For example, you can hypothesise that one day we will discover a way of breaking the speed of light barrier. Although this contradicts Relativity, it is conceivable (although not necessarily likely or even possible) that one day we will formulate a more general theory that admits superluminal speed under specific circumstances not considered in Relativity, exactly as Relativity generalises Newtonian Mechanics without invalidate it.

Sometimes, a HSF story speculates on possible consequences of what we already know. Some other times, it relies on a new discovery to trigger a chain of events. But, in any case, it remains consistent to its premises.

Arthur C. Clarke, one of the greatest HSF authors of all times, formulated three laws to help people predict the future:

1. When a distinguished but elderly scientist states that something is possible, he is almost certainly right. When he states that something is impossible, he is very probably wrong.

2. The only way of discovering the limits of the possible is to venture a little way past them into the impossible.

3. Any sufficiently advanced technology is indistinguishable from magic.

The difference between Clarke's third law and the magic found in so many books sold today is that the magic Clarke refers to is perceived, not real. If somebody of even just a couple of hundred years ago could visit today's world, would see spells and charms where there are none.

I am a Trekker, a convinced Star Trek fan. Gene Roddenberry's stories rely on three things that, when Star Trek was first aired, were considered impossible: warp drive, transporters, and artificial gravity. They were "tricks" to make the stories possible. Without superluminal speed, travel between the stars would have taken many years, too long for 45-minute episodes; transporters made landing onto alien worlds easy, as always shuttling forth and back would have been bothersome and time consuming; and artificial gravity was necessary for two reasons: a film with people constantly floating around would have been annoying to say the least, and the acceleration of a starship would have killed the crew.

I don't remember who said that in a good HSF story, you can ask the reader to believe something that is considered impossible, but only once. And yet, although Star Trek expected from us to suspend disbelief more than once, those stories inspired real astronauts and scientists, and it is no longer clear that faster than light travel will remain impossible forever.

Without HSF, where would future generations of scientists find their inspirations? Who would tell them stories about all those impossible things they can aim for?

Originally posted in my blog on 2012-07-04.

The World as I see it

Misunderstood Science: A question of probability

Probability and statistics are very confusing. Most people think they are self evident and consider them easy to handle, at least in everyday's life. But they are wrong. For starters, how many of you could state the difference between probability and statistics?

No?

OK. Here it is: probabilities are decided in advance and have to do with predicting possible outcomes while statistics are concerned with inferring the likelyhood of possible events based on observed outcomes.

For example, if you have a six-faced die and state that each face will come up on average once every six throws, you are talking about probabilities: you estimate probabilities in advance with a mathematical formula and use them to predict what you might get in practice.

If, on the other hand, throw a six-faced die 600 times and count how many times each face comes up in an attempt to determine how probable they are, you are doing statistics. Obviously, statistics cannot ever be an exact science.

For one thing, no die can be perfectly balanced. Even if you started with a perfectly balanced die (and you tell me how you would determine that!), you couldn't keep it that way because with each throw imperceptible abrasions would remove tiny particles (perhaps just atoms) from one or more faces. All in all, if you throw any die enough times, you will discover that some faces come up, on average, more often than others.

But even with an ideal, perfectly balanced die (which, I repeat, is a physical impossibility), you cannot expect to get all faces exactly the same number of times. It is theoretically possible but, the higher the number of throws, the less likely it is. If you throw a die, say, 600 times, I bet you a thousand dollars against ten that you will spend the rest of your life trying to get 100 1s, 100 2s, etc. (I'll settle the matter with your heirs).

How do you calculate a probability? Conceptually, it is simple: The probability of an outcome is given by the number of ways in which you can obtain that outcome divided by the total number of ways in which you can obtain all possible outcomes. That's why it is easy to estimate that the probability of, say, a 5 when throwing a die is 1/6 (~16.7%), or the probability of head when throwing a coin is 1/2 (50.0%).

FYI, statisticians call the set of all possible outcomes the sample space. This is a bit twisted because sample is a statistical term, while sample space refers to the calculation of probabilities, but who says that scientists are always consistent?

Anyhow, the concept of sample space and the above definition of probability lets you answer questions like: what is the probability of getting a 10 if I throw two dice?

The size of the sample space is 36 because you can get 6 possible values with each dice, and they are independent from each other. The possible ways in which you can obtain a 10 are: (4,6), (5,5), and (6,4). As a result, the probability of obtaining a 10 is 3/36 (~ 8.3%). As a comparison, you can obtain a 7 with (1,6), (2,5), (3,4), (4,3), (5,2) and (6,1), which results in a probability of 6/36 (~16.7%).

Everything clear? Let's check it out with a fun problem.

I place a ten-dollar bill in one of three identical boxes. Then, while you keep your eyes closed, I move them around so that I still know where the money is but you lose track of it. You have to choose one of the boxes; if it is the box with the money, the ten dollars are your. Clearly, you have a probability of 1/3 (or ~33.3%) to win. You make your choice by placing your hand on one of the boxes. But, before you can open your box, I open one of the other two boxes and show you that it is empty. I then ask you whether you want to stick to your original choice or switch to the other box that is still unopened. What do you do and why?

Obviously, you want to maximise the probability of winning. The questions you need to answer are: does it matter whether you keep the box you initially chose or you switch to the other box that is still unopened? And if it does matter, are you more likely to win if you keep the original box or if you swap it for the other one?

The answer seems obvious: there are two boxes and only one contains a reward. As there are no reasons for preferring either box, it seems irrelevant which one you choose. They both have a 50/50 chance of being the winning one.

Or not?

Well, ... no. You are better off switching boxes because the other unopened box is more likely to contain the ten-dollar bill than the one you initially chose.

Surprised? Let's see...

What is the probability that you chose the winning box? As I already said: 1/3. If you keep the box, you also keep the 33.3% chance of winning.

And what is the probability that the money is in one of the two boxes you didn't choose? Obviously, 2/3. But I have already opened one of the two other boxes and showed to you that it was empty. Therefore, the probability that the reward is the box I haven't opened remains 2/3.

In conclusion, if you stick with your original choice, you keep your initial 1/3 probability of winning, but if you switch boxes after I have opened one of the unchosen ones, you have a 2/3 probability of winning. Twice as high!

Where is the trick?

There is no trick. The whole story appears illogical only because of a widespread fallacy incurred by many people when thinking about probabilities. For probabilities to be equally spread among different outcomes, the possible outcomes must be *independent* from each other. In our game, they initially were independent, but ceased to be so when I opened one of the boxes. This is because *I knew* that the box was empty. This made the content of the third box no longer independent. If I had opened one of the boxes without knowing whether it was empty or not, the probability of finding the money in either your box or in the third box would have been equally spread at 50/50, as you probably thought.

If you are not convinced, think that if I had opened one of the two boxes without knowing that it was empty, I would have had 1/3 of probability of opening the winning box, exactly the same probability you had when choosing your box. But if that had not happened, and I had opened an empty box without knowing in advance that it was empty, I would have not introduced any dependency because opening that box would have not said anything about the third box.

Amazing, isn't it? Martin Gardner once said: *in no other branch of Mathematics is it so easy for experts to blunder as in probability theory*. Imagine for non-experts...

Originally posted in my blog on 2012-11-12.

Creativity and Research

Sue North, in her PhD thesis titled *Relations of Power and Competing Knowledges Within the Academy: Creative Writing as Research* (University of Canberra, 2004), writes:

> *The doxa of creative work and the doxa of research arise from different epistemological underpinnings – creativity from the unexplainable force of the imagination, and research from the logical force of understanding.*[1]

In simple terms, she said that it is common knowledge that creativity is a manifestation of imagination, while research is a process based on studying, understanding, and logical thinking. By using the word doxa, she tells us that these beliefs are so widely accepted that they don't even need to be expressed. In other words, everybody considers them to be true.

I agree with her: most people think that way. But I believe that they do so because they don't have a clear understanding of how people tap their creativity and what it means to do research.

The concepts that artists pull their creations out of thin air and that researchers only exercise logic are both wrong.

Let's look at artists first. They couldn't create anything without studying the world around them, the work of other artists, and the tools they need in order to do their work. Ideas don't just spring out of the mind of an artist fully clothed and armed, like Athena out of Jupiter's head.

As an example, consider what writing a novel involves.

---

[1] *Doxa* is a common belief or popular opinion, while *Epistemology* is the branch of philosophy concerned with knowledge.

The World as I see it

The author needs to invent characters and design a plot for them, so that they can interact with each other. Some authors start with a plot and others starts with the characters, but, in either case, they must ensure that those two elements are consistent and credible (and interesting :-). This can only come after years of observing how people interact and trying to understand what motivates them.

And then, authors cannot write their novels with any hope of success unless they know their craft: structure, voice, pace, dialogue, to name some aspects of it. This means that they need to learn techniques, read a lot, and write a lot.

Creative Writing is the Cinderella of Academia. This status of affairs reflects the almost universal opinion that, because everybody can write, studying Creative Writing is a trivial activity pursued by people who want to have it easy at the University.

It is only when people actually try to write something worth reading that they realise how little they know and how much they need to work in order to get any recognition.

Furthermore, to write a novel an author needs logic, discipline, and rigour, otherwise his/her few hundred pages will be full of inconsistencies, loose threads, and untruths.

In order to create realistic characters placed in a realistic environment and doing realistic actions, an author needs to do a lot of research. Most (I would say all, but I don't want to be so absolute) authors define their characters and their plots to a level of detail that remains below the surface of the finished product. What ends up into the novel is only the tip of the iceberg.

Authors also perform another activity typical of research: experimentation. This can be in the content, the dialogue, or the form. For example, Peter Carey, in his historical novel

True History of the Kelly Gang, doesn't use a single comma, while Alessandro Baricco, in his short novel *Silk*, uses line breaks to control the pace and convey meaning. And if this seems too literary and abstract, how much research do you think Frank Herbert had to do in order to create the universe in which his Dune stories take place?

I'm talking about creative writing because I had a couple of non-fiction books and a couple of Science Fiction stories published. Therefore, I can base my reasoning on some experience. But I'm sure that equivalent concepts apply to other creative activities.

I hope I have convinced you that creative work couldn't exist without logical thinking, knowledge, and research. If not, read again what I just say and reflect more on it.

Now, let's look at scientific research. I shall go out on a limb here and say that without imagination any type of research would be impossible.

It is standard practice in academic papers to present the results of research in a logical fashion: you write about existing results, identify a gap, and explain how your results close it. There is more to it but, in essence, research papers are logical to the core. This is especially true in Physics, the prototypical scientific discipline.

But this is not how research actually works. Most neatly presented conclusions are in reality the result of hunches, insights, leaps, backtracking, crises, and serendipitous events (i.e., strokes of luck). Research works somewhat like solving a jigsaw puzzle: you start from the edges and the pieces you can easily recognise. Then, you fill the gaps to complete the picture. Sometimes, you feel that a piece might be right in a certain spot and place it there, hoping to have it confirmed later. But both academic papers for the scientific community and magazine articles for the rest of us present the research process as if the researchers had started the puzzle from the top-left corner and systematically worked their way to the bottom-right piece.

The key point I'm trying to express is that logic cannot add knowledge. It can be used to extract information that for any reason is still hidden in the data and, sometimes, this leads to surprising and useful results, which in turn can trigger new avenues of research. But, ultimately, truly new discoveries occur when a researcher follows a hunch and jumps over a gap in the logic. This is what Edward De Bono calls *Lateral Thinking*. And what about the creativity that any experimental researcher needs in order to overcome the many technical (e non-technical) problems [s]he encounters daily?

In other words, imagination plays an essential role in the progress of Science and Technology. The logical chain of thought is often reconstructed after the discovery has been made or a working solution found. When a scientist gets enamoured with an idea and invents an experiment to verify it, [s]he will not necessarily tell you. Think of Einstein and his special theory of relativity. He postulated the constancy of the speed of light. He certainly didn't deduce it logically.

To conclude, successful creative endeavours require study, understanding, and logic, while scientific research produces its best results thanks to insights, imagination, and dedication. So, please, let's stop perpetuating these stereotypes of wild artists and white-coated scientists!

Originally posted in my blog on 2013-02-25.

The World as I see it
Reflections on Faith and Science

I am an atheist. No doubt about it. I don't believe that some all-powerful, self-conscious entity is interested in our lives or even that such an entity exists. There are no reasons for believing that a God exists, but neither are there reasons for not believing that it exists. Therefore, the most logical position is to be an agnostic, not an atheist. I should be able to say: I neither believe nor disbelieve. And yet, I don't believe. For somebody like me, who has a scientific formation, this is not completely satisfying, because I am asserting something that can be neither proven nor disproven.

In any case, the existence or non-existence of God doesn't affect my life in any way. At least not directly, as what believers manage to impose on everybody else does have an influence on me. Religious fervour has resulted in laws prohibiting abortion (like in Malta and Chile[1]), traditions keeping girls out of school (like in Afghanistan), and regulations forcing restrictive dress codes on women (like in the Orthodox Jewish quarter of Tel Aviv, where women must cover their arms). Obviously, I will never need an abortion, I have been able to attend school, and I am allowed to wear short-sleeved shirts wherever I want. Nevertheless, these rules, often directed at women, are deeply annoying.

But this distinction between atheism and agnosticism is just another way of placing people in boxes. A more important distinction is whether people have doubts or not. Certainties are dangerous. Certainties make possible for fanatics to strap around their waists belts full of explosive and blow themselves up in public places. Certainties have caused over the whole recorded history of Humanity persecutions of entire ethnics groups and tortures of millions.

---

1 At least when I wrote this article in 2013.

In fact, I believe that certainties are responsible for most of the problems we have today. There are too many faithfuls and not enough scientists.

What many non-scientists have difficulties in grasping is that *no scientific statement can ever be proven to be absolutely true.*[1] For example, Newton's theory of gravitation worked flawlessly for a long time and is still used every day. But it was discovered that it couldn't fully explain the orbit of the planet Mercury. Einstein's theory of gravitation solved that problem and has been confirmed by countless measurements. Does it mean that Newton was wrong? Not at all. It only means that Newton's theory is an approximation of general relativity or, if you prefer, that Einstein's theory can explain a wider class of phenomena and with more accuracy. Does it mean that Einstein's theory will always be right? Again, not at all. It only means that, so far, it has never been proven to be at fault (although, truth be told, general relativity has not been successfully integrated with quantum mechanics; but that's another story).

Scientific statements, therefore, are never-ending works-in-progress. That is, they can be proven wrong in some cases, but the proof of their correctness never ends. Despite of their intrinsic uncertainties, all these temporary laws of Physics can still be used to discover further laws that explain our universe. It is a bit like crossing an infinitely wide mountain creek on wobbling stones: scientists keep stepping on the same wobbly theories and, as they progress, the older theories become more and more trustworthy; more stable paths are identified.

People who insist that Intelligent Design (ID) should be taught at school in Science classes as an alternative to Evolution by Natural Selection (ENS) can only do so because

---

[1] As I already explained in a preceding article, which has some overlapping with this one.

most people don't know what I have explained in the previous two paragraphs. The ID people state that ENS is an unproven theory. But *there is no scientific theory completely proven*. It is impossible. The key issue is that ENS can be disproven, while ID cannot. That is why ENS is a scientific theory and ID is not!

The same problem pops up with the hoopla about climate change, levels of CO_2, and whether the changes are anthropic or not. People ignorant in Science would like to have clear, unambiguous, and final answers, and confuse scientific results with beliefs. But certainty has no place in Science.

My attitude towards God is scientific: if, after asking me whether I believe that a God exists (to which, as I said, I would reply no), you asked me whether I'm sure, I would have to answer with another no. Of course I'm not sure. How could I? But I don't need to introduce an "ad hock" entity that explains everything Science cannot [yet] understand. For centuries, the Catholic Church was a drag on Science because it wanted to cling to its revealed truths (actually, it still is). It was (is) a problem caused by certainties (not "misplaced certainties", because all certainties are misplaced).

All so-called proofs of the existence of God that come to mind rely on negatives: all this beauty of nature cannot be the result of random events; we don't know how our universe came into existence; it cannot be that our existence has no purpose; etc. But how can one claim to prove anything on the basis of what one doesn't know? It is baffling.

I know little about Judaism and Islam (I confess I am somewhat ashamed of my ignorance), but I was taught the Catholic catechism[1]. I strongly encourage you to have a look at it, especially if you have never done it before. It is an amazing construction of cross-linked concepts. I have to

---

1 http://www.vatican.va/archive/ENG0015/_INDEX.HTM

wonder how many so-called faithfuls actually believe much of what is in there...

As Alain de Botton convincingly explained in his book *Religion for Atheists*[1], religion has its functions and its usefulness in society. But it should be kept in check and not overpower everything else.

Christianity might have shaped morality and laws of the western world, but I don't need a priest to tell me that to contribute to a harmonious society I should behave with others as I would like them to behave with me. Luke's "do to others as you would have them do to you" (verse 6:31) is only an expression of a Golden Rule[2] that has been recognised and applied in many cultures since antiquity.

I believe that ENS has resulted in the collaborative attitude of human beings. A typical example of such a "social" attitude is shown by how people behave when confronted with the game called "the prisoner's dilemma". From Wikipedia (look in particular to the last sentence):

Two members of a criminal gang are arrested and imprisoned. Each prisoner is in solitary confinement with no means of speaking to or exchanging messages with the other. The police admit they don't have enough evidence to convict the pair on the principal charge. They plan to sentence both to a year in prison on a lesser charge. Simultaneously, the police offer each prisoner a Faustian bargain. Each prisoner is given the opportunity either to betray the other, by testifying that the other committed the crime, or to cooperate with the other by remaining silent. Here's how it goes:

- *If A and B both betray the other, each of them serves 2 years in prison*

---

1 https://www.alaindebotton.com/religion/

2 https://en.wikipedia.org/wiki/Golden_Rule

- *If A betrays B but B remains silent, A will be set free and B will serve 3 years in prison (and vice versa)*
- *If A and B both remain silent, both of them will only serve 1 year in prison (on the lesser charge)*

It's implied that the prisoners will have no opportunity to reward or punish their partner in addition to the prison sentences they get, and that their decision won't affect their reputation in future. Because betraying a partner offers a greater reward than cooperating with them, all purely rational self-interested prisoners would betray the other [...]. The interesting part of this result is that pursuing individual reward logically leads both of the prisoners to betray, when they would get a better reward if they both cooperated. In reality, humans display a systematic bias towards cooperative behavior in this and similar games, much more so than predicted by simple models of "rational" self-interested action.

It makes sense to speak of rules of ethics applicable to everyone, but, except for predispositions resulting from ENS, they ought to be based on rationality, with the aim of maximising our collective well-being, not allegedly inspired by an imagined God invented to comfort us. There is no need for a God to explain the validity of moral codes.

For millennia, religions played an important role in constraining some of human emotions that, if uncontrolled, would have resulted in chaos. But, at the same time, religions also exploited those same emotions for their own purposes of expansion and control. I say: let's get rid of them!

We must invest as much as possible in education, so that a secular, conscious morality will eventually replace the rules imposed by superstition, regardless of whether it is called witchcraft or religion. One day, with the help of Science, we will be able to control our destructive emotions rationally, while still enjoying the positive ones. Only then, we will have left behind the caves of our ancestors and be ready to explore the universe.

Originally posted in my blog on 2013-12-31.

READING AND WRITING

The World as I see it

Copyright, Copyleft, and Copywrong

The Free Software Foundation (FSF) founded by Richard Stallman decades ago is based on the idea that software users should be able to collaborate with each other. Proprietary software, with its restrictions imposed by its copyright holders, makes that impossible. Users should be able to run the software, study it, modify it, and redistribute it.

To provide an alternative to the proprietary versions of the Unix operating system, Stallman started the GNU project[1], which, together with Linus Torvalds' Linux kernel, resulted in what everybody today calls the Linux operating system (which should actually be called GNU/Linux, but few bother).[2]

GNU/Linux (I do bother) is a great achievement, and thousands of developers have contributed to its success by extending it, maintaining, and adding to it useful applications.

FSF software is free for everyone to use, adapt, and redistribute, but only as long as the modified or repackaged software remains free. To achieve this, the software is licensed with what is called a copyleft, of which the standard GNU licence is a particular version.

Stallman is an extremely intelligent person, an inspired speaker, and totally dedicated to the free software movement. His ideas are contagious, and he has my admiration, but the fact that he believes in what he says, or even that many believe in what he says, doesn't automatically mean that what he says is right for you and me.

---

1 GNU is a recursive acronym and stands for "Gnu is Not Unix"

2 FYI, this book is being edited on Ubuntu Linux.

The World as I see it

Like with every social or political movement, there are, broadly speaking, two types of people who favour the free software movement: the true believers and the opportunists.

The true believers deserve our respect. They put a lot of effort into developing software to see it "fly". Their reward is to know that thousands or millions of people around the world use what they have developed. They keep learning and love to discuss the intricacies of their products with like-minded people.

The opportunists are those who are against proprietary software because they like to get as much as possible for free. On the basis of what I have learnt about human nature, I wouldn't be surprised to discover that, unfortunately, they are the vast majority.

By misusing the ideals of the FSF, they can take the high moral ground and portray themselves as people who fight the rich and allegedly corrupt multinationals (e.g., Microsoft and Apple). What better excuse is there for obtaining pirated copies of proprietary programs than an act of civil justice?

Allow me to be sceptical about moral choices that benefit the person who takes them.

Where do you stop? Everybody knows that the government is corrupt. Why should we then pay taxes? And the supermarkets exploit the farmers and make too much profit on what they sell. Isn't then justified to "appropriate" stuff from their shelves? In Italy, in the early 1970s, when one third of the population voted for the Communist party, we even had a term for it: *spesa proletaria* (i.e., proletarian shopping).

Give me a break!

Do these abuses invalidate the FSF ideals? Of course not, but millions and millions of people have found in it a justification for stealing. And, perhaps not surprisingly, the idea of free software has contributed to the concept of "free everything". The prevailing culture today is that it is OK to "share" some songs, even if "sharing" has become a euphemism for downloading hundred of songs for free. And scripts, books, and films are sometimes available for download within days of their release.

But make no mistake: downloading illegal copies of any copyrighted material is stealing.

In 2007 I published an IT book with a list price of US$40, but Amazon sells it for about US$26 in printed form and for less than USD$18 as an eBook. For prices that I consider moderate, you get almost 450 pages of very specialised material. And yet, you can download free pirated or scanned copies of the book from several websites.

Whom are we kidding? Those who deprive authors like me of a couple of dollars of royalties per copy are not heroic people who fight their quixotic battle against the multinationals. They are thieves.

The downloading of pirated music is to a large extent to blame for the current crisis affecting the music industry, and the publishing industry is next.

Few authors, musicians, actors, and directors make a living from their artistic endeavours, and even fewer become rich. Piracy is an additional unnecessary hurdle that emerging artists, developers, and small independent publishers need to overcome.

And, just that I am at it, not only do I think that copyright is perfectly justified and should be enforced. I also think that it shouldn't expire.

If you build a house or a company, you can pass it on to your heirs in perpetuity. Once your heirs will have paid the necessary taxes, fees, succession taxes, and what have you, they will own the physical results of your work. Marx said that property is theft, but Communism didn't work, did it?

The same happens with less tangible goods, like shares, bonds, and plain old cash.

But if you invest your time and effort in producing intellectual property, your heirs will lose all their rights 70 years after your death. Now, 70 years seem a long period of time, but can you imagine applying the same to a farm or to a factory, or even to a painting or a sculpture? Can you imagine that one day some government official will knock on the door of your great-grandchildren and evict them from the house you have built because it is no longer theirs? I don't think so.

In which way is intellectual property different from brick and mortar? Isn't a fundamental doctrine of Economics that higher risk should be rewarded with higher yield? And what is more risky than writing a book?

You might resent the fact that a book keeps generating royalties long after the author is dead, without the need for any additional effort. But wait a minute! What about the dividends you get from shares and the interests you get from bank deposits? Isn't it the same?

Most books stop selling after a few years. Books in print and being sold longer than 70 years after the author's death are rare exceptions. Therefore, an unlimited copyright would only make a difference for the few "classics". And for those, to reiterate my point, why shouldn't the heirs benefit from them?

There is also another aspect to consider: when a copyright is extinguished, it is not just the royalties that disappear. The copyright holder loses any control he previously had. This means that anybody will be entitled to re-publish the book (or the song) with any alteration he might like to make! That seems completely preposterous. A dictator might decide to adapt a text to support his ideas. In fact there is a never-ending debate about whether the spelling of some old text should be adapted to "freshen up" centuries-old books.

Now, I know that the Constitution of the United States states that copyright should expire but, as Mark Twain once suggested, why not setting it to a million years? That would be constitutional, wouldn't it?

Originally posted in my blog on 2012-07-31.

The World as I see it

The World as I see it

Category Romance Novels

Category (or Series) Romance novels are those small and inexpensive paperbacks with sweet and happy couples portrayed on the front cover. You find them in stores like K-Mart and Target but seldom in bookshops.

Famous historical novels like *Gone with the Wind* are not Category Romance novels. The love story between Rhett and Scarlett is central to *Gone with the Wind*, but is not its only theme. Category novels are much more narrowly focussed on the relationship between their protagonists.

Romance novels are about love relationships. The tradition, started by Jane Austen with her romantic novels set in the Regency Era (1811-1820), endures, but the modern romance novels have developed far beyond the intrigues and the rich dresses of British aristocracy of the early 1800s. To convince yourself how true such a statement is, you only need to look at the web site of Mills & Boon / Harlequin, the best known publishers of Category Romance. Harlequin is a Canadian publisher that acquired M&B (a UK publisher) some decades ago.

Before I talk about Romance Writing, let me give you some figures, which I got from Wikipedia[1]. In 2008, M&B sold 200 million novels per year, and is currently publishing about 100 books and 100 e-books per month. Harlequin is currently releasing 120 new titles each month in 29 different languages and in 107 international markets. In the UK alone, M&B has over 3 million regular readers. If you thought that Romance novels were a niche market, think again!

---

1 These are figures of 2013, but I didn't bother to update them because I believe that they are sufficient for the sake of this article.

The World as I see it

I will reproduce here how M&B defines the characteristics of some of their series (i.e., imprints), extracted from the Australian submission guidelines. They publish several books in each imprint every month.

Sexy: These stories are all about passion and escape, glamorous international settings, captivating women and the seductive, tempting men who want them. Length: 50,000 words. Spine colour: red.

Sweet Romance: Sweet Romance stories are all about real, relatable women and strong, deeply desirable men experiencing the intensity, anticipation and sheer rush of falling in love. Length: 50,000 words. Spine colour: light blue.

Medical: Intense and uplifting romances set in the medical world. Experience the breath-taking rollercoaster of emotions, ambitions and desires of today's medical professionals. Length: 50,000 words. Spine colour: teal.

Historical: Richly textured, emotionally intense novels set across a wide range of historical periods - ancient civilisations up to and including the Second World War. Length: 65,000 words. Spine colour: blue.

Blaze: Blaze is Mills & Boon's sexiest romance series, yet there's more to these books than simply sex. We ask our authors to deliver complex plots and subplots, realistic engaging characters and a consuming love story you won't be able to forget. Blaze stories are fun, flirty and always steamy! Length: 60,000 words. Spine colour: orange.

Blush: Are big romance novels filled with intense relationships, real life drama and the kinds of unexpected events that change women's lives forever! Length: 85,000 words. Featuring relatable characters who strike a chord with the reader regardless of the book's setting or plot points. Length: 55,000-60,000 words. Spine colour: purple.

Intrigue: Crime stories tailored to the series romance market packed with a variety of thrilling suspense and whodunit mystery. Length: 55,000-60,000 words. Spine colour: dark blue.

Desire: Contemporary, sensual, conflict-driven romances that feature strong-but-vulnerable alpha heroes and dynamic heroines who want love - and more! Reads that are always powerful, passionate and provocative. Length: 50,000-55,000 words. Spine colour: pink.

Romantic Suspense: These novels are romance-focused stories with a suspense element. Powerful romances are at the heart of each story, and the additional elements of excitement, adventure and suspense play out between complex characters. Length: 70,000-75,000 words. Spine colour: dark purple.

Nocturne: Dark, sexy, atmospheric paranormal romances that feature larger-than-life characters struggling with life-and-death issues. Length: 80,000-85,000 words. Spine colour: black.

As you can see, you can find all sorts of Romance novels. Ultimately, they are all meant to transport a lady reader to a world of fantasy in which Good always prevails over Evil. Harlequin has similar guidelines. But Harlequin also has a series of e-books, "Historical Undone", with a length of between 10,000 and 15,000 words. This could be a good entry point to test the waters before writing and submitting a full-length novel.

The series that I find more congenial is "Sweet Romance". This is because the novels are short (50,000 words) and don't include explicit sex. It's not that I am so puritanical, but I don't like to read about "sliding members" and "penetrating male sexes".

I had never read Category Romance novels before discovering that they have such a huge market and, for a while, I warmed up to the idea of writing Romance stories.

Here is my recipe for writing a successful "Sweet Romance" novel, taken from the writings of Valerie Parv and Emma Darcy, two very successful Romance authors.

Characters

If there is a character-centred genre, this is Romance.

- Romance novels essentially have two characters: the heroine and the hero. All other characters are only there for support and shouldn't do much.

- The protagonist must the heroine. She must be beautiful, intelligent, honest, and successful. This doesn't mean that she must be perfect, but almost. In essence, she must be somebody with whom any woman might like to identify.

- The hero must appeal to the vast majority of Romance readers. Therefore, he must be handsome, sexy, A-male. But he should also be not much younger and not much older than the heroine and (obviously) honest, courageous, and generous. In essence, every reader should be able to vicariously fall in love with him. Incidentally, surveys have proven that the readers prefer dark-haired heroes.

- The protagonists never engage in casual sex, never steal, and never use violence. It used to be that the protagonist needed to be a virgin, but this is no longer strictly necessary, although it is not appropriate to dwell on previous sexual relationships of the protagonists.

- If the hero does something "naughty" like telling a lie or getting drunk, you have to explain in detail why and show that he is in fact a good man and at once feeling guilty for committing such a bad act. You should also make clear that it is a one off and that it will never happen again. Best, don't make him do anything you then have to waste pages and pages of contrition in order to recover from.

- No swearwords, ever!

- No physical features that would make it impossible for the reader to identify with the heroine. That is, the heroine must not be too tall or too short, with a weight problem or anorexic, etc.

Plot

- The plot should be linear. Forget flashbacks and memories. They only distract from what is happening now.

- At least in the "standard" 50,000-word novel, no subplots. There is not enough space for them and, in any case, they distract from the main plot.

- The protagonist and the hero should already meet in the first chapter. Possibly, in the very first paragraph.

- There must be at least one major conflict between the protagonist and the hero, and this must become clear as soon as possible. Ideally when they meet. This conflict (supported perhaps by a couple of additional minor issues) is what keeps the protagonists apart, even if they feel attracted to each other immediately.

- The main plot is the evolution of the relationship between the protagonist and the hero and the ultimate resolution of the conflict between them. The relationship should go through two or three crises, of increasing seriousness, alternating with peaks of happiness/optimism, to reach a satisfyingly happy ending.

- The protagonists marry in the last chapter, with a very short resolution, if any. This implies that you must resolve all minor issues and tie up all loose ends before you resolve the main conflict and bring the protagonists fully together. Note that love, at least in Romance novels, is forever.

- Nowadays, they can have full intercourse before marrying, but it shouldn't happen too early in the novel. This is because intimacy is something to achieve, and only when it is clear that the protagonists are in love. Make them do it too soon, and you will struggle to hold them apart until they finally unite at the end.

General Points

- As the readership consists almost exclusively of women, you must not write what a woman is likely to find distasteful, especially if it refers to the protagonist.

- The point of view must be that of the protagonist. You can briefly switch to the point of view of the hero, but only if strictly necessary to support the plot and only briefly and clearly. In other words, omniscient and multiple viewpoints are out.

- You have to maintain pace throughout the novel. This is done through dialogues and by surprising or shocking the reader. Suspense and short chapters help. Try to end each chapter with something that might encourage the reader to start the next one. These are short books, and many readers go through one of them every day.

- Try to set the novel in a stimulating environment. Incidentally, novels set in the Australian Outback seem to be quite successful with American readers.

- Do not waste many words on the scenery. Ultimately, the readers are interested in the characters, and in particular the heroine, more than on anything else.

- Narrative should be kept to a minimum. Some readers page through books and buy those that contain more dialogue.

- Like with any other form of writing, remorselessly cut down anything that doesn't advance the plot or help developing the characters. With only 50,000 available, you cannot afford long-winded descriptions or speeches.

- Limit each chapter to about 20 pages, so that the whole book consists of 10 to 12 chapters.

- Use short sentences in small paragraphs. A lot of ink without breaks is usually discouraging.

- If you are a man, use a female pen name and invent a persona to go with it because almost no reader will think that a male author can create a good female fantasy.

To write successful novels, you always have to conform to what the readers want, and the readers of Category Romance have very strict requirements. You can see this as a straightjacket or as a challenge. It's up to you!

Originally posted in my blog on 2012-09-15.

The World as I see it

The World as I see it

More than One Way of Reading

I have been reading *How to Talk about Books You Haven't Read*, a book written by the French psychoanalyst and professor of literature Pierre Bayard. It is small but full of interesting ideas.

Bayard convincingly makes the point that "reading" has not a single, universally applicable meaning, and challenges us to admit that sometimes (or often, or always) we talk about books that we haven't read from cover to cover.

Furthermore, he points out that, inevitably, we only retain a fraction of the information contained in a book. Therefore, even if we have indeed carefully read a book in its entirety, we can only talk about our impressions and interpretations that its content has elicited in us.

And as our memories fade with time, can we knowledgeably talk about books that we read months and years ago?

This last point stroke a chord with me. In a couple of occasions, I even bought a book I had already read, thinking that I hadn't. It was somewhat bewildering to discover another copy of the same book in my bookcase. If I can completely forget some of the books I read, I have certainly forgotten the content of many of the books I still remember to have read.

What is the length of the reading-forgetting cycle? For me, scaringly short. I used to have a very good memory. I could read a poem a few times and be able to recite it. But, with the passing of years, my short- and medium-term memories have been deteriorating. Sometimes, immediately after reading a novel, I wonder how it begun. And my memory for names, whether they are characters in a story of real people in real life, is simply appalling.

Hopefully, something of what I read is still spread across a number of neurons and influences my thought.

On the basis of these considerations, why should I be more entitled to talk about a book I read long ago than somebody who skimmed it a couple of days ago or recently read an article about it?

It really seems that "reading" is in the eye of the beholder, to paraphrase a well known cliché.

Bayard suggests that we qualify each book with an acronym that indicates its "reading status":

- UB   book unknown to me
- SB   book I have skimmed
- HB   book I have heard about
- FB   book I have forgotten

It seems reasonable, but I contend that UB is totally useless because, as soon as somebody mentions to me a book I didn't know it existed, that book immediately acquires for me the status HB. Then, what's the purpose of defining the status UB? Perhaps Bayard reserves UB for books of which he only knows the title, or part of it, but that doesn't make sense because the title already tells something about the content. UB could only be used for all books of which I don't even know the titles, but I certainly don't care about them.

I also have a small issue with FB, because you can only forget what you once knew. So, does FB apply to books that were once SB or HB? And what about the books we actually read (in the strictest sense of reading all words in them)?

Notice that Bayard doesn't define any acronym for books actually read. This is because he considers "read" too ambiguous to be used (or perhaps because he never really reads any book). But I like to think that if I have actually read more than 50% of the pages of a book, and have not forgotten of its existence, I should be able to use RB. Obviously, with time, many RBs will silently morph into FBs.

I religiously (interesting spontaneous choice of adverb...) maintain a list of all books I own, once owned, and/or have read. There are books I own and have read, books I own and haven't read [yet], books I read but don't own (either because I borrowed them or because I gave them away), and books I don't own and have never read. The last category only includes a handful of books I want to remember for whatever reasons. Consistently with what I said in the previous paragraph, I flag a book as "read" if I actually read at least 50% of its pages.

All in all, the classification I find most appropriate (if there has to be one) is as follows:

- HB   book I have heard of or read about but never held in my hands
- SB   book I have held in my hands and skimmed
- RB   book of which I once read more than 50% of the pages

Whether I have forgotten what I once knew about the book or not, refers to a totally different dimension and applies to all books I came in contact with, regardless of the way in which that happened.

Originally posted in my blog on 2013-04-19.

The World as I see it

The Book Lives On

When I finally bought an iPad, I was looking forward to reading a lot of books that were no longer in print. I warmed at the idea that one day I could take with me all the books I had ever read.

But I then discovered that the iPad was too heavy for comfort when reading in bed, where I do a non-negligible part of my reading. And holding it by the edge meant that sometimes I would unintentionally flip a page. Furthermore, sometimes I wanted to reflect on what I had just read or re-read a paragraph, and that resulted in a dimming of the display. As Captain Picard said in the Star Trek The Next Generation episode *Yesterday's Enterprise* (one of my favourite), *Not good enough, dammit, not good enough!*

And yet, as Sherman Young convincingly affirms in his book *The book is dead*, the only way for the book to survive is if book lovers embrace eBooks.

Young's book was published in 2007, three years before the iPad became available (2010-04-03 in the USA). Therefore, Young's vision of a heavenly library was still an act of faith. He wrote:

> *We can imagine the heavenly library as the world's collection of books available in an instant. It will be searchable, downloadable, readable with recommendations and suggestions from other readers, authors and critics; and a place to contribute to discussions about the book in question. Imagine that it will allow access to titles that might not be feasible in print (one in which all the Vogel shortlisters are published, not just the winner); where the new Patrick Whites get to hang out their talent for as many books as is required to find their voice. Imagine a catalogue of*

> *niches, made possible and searchable via electronic delivery; enabling a different set of publishing economics and priorities.*

Does it sound familiar? We are definitely getting there. No more trees felled; no more money spent on printing books and shipping them around the world; no more books out of print; no more well-written books full of ideas that remain unpublished because they are systematically rejected.

Sherman points out that the term *book* has come to identify both a physical object consisting of bound printed pages and its conceptual content of information and ideas. In his opinion, and I agree with him, we should distinguish between the two meanings.

There are many objects like telephone books, dictionaries, cookbooks, travel books, puzzle books, etc. that, although they consist of bounded printed pages, do not communicate any ideas, do not make the readers reflect on what they are reading, and do not contribute to a book culture that involves exchanging opinions and experiences with others. Such objects effectively are *non-books*.

Other borderline non-books are most of those written by celebrities, regardless of whether they are performers (actors, sportspeople, politicians, etc.) or individuals who gained fame or notoriety by executing some news-making acts, like circumnavigating the world solo or killing somebody.

From a practical point of view, what the non-books have in common is that they are designed to make quick money for the publishers. Publishers used to invest in promising authors and then nurture them to success, but today's big publishers (and most of the small publishers as well) are an industry like any other. It doesn't make any difference to them that they are selling books instead of vacuum cleaners. What counts is that they can show good quarterly figures. In a sense, we cannot even blame them, because the whole society is fixed on making a quick buck.

Fortunately, the Internet and electronic publishing give us a new way of sustaining a book culture (and culture in general). Those with ideas can express them and communicate them to like-minded people living anywhere in the world.

According to Chris Anderson (*The Long Tail*, p 127), "the future of business is selling less of more". What he means in practical terms is that businesses can make more money by selling few instances of many items than by selling lots of instances of few items. In his book, published in 2006, Anderson concentrated on the music industry, but what he wrote applies to eBooks as well.

To understand how this works, consider this: if 10 titles sell in one year 1,000,000 copies, they result in the sale of 10 million books; if, at the same time, 1,000,000 titles sell 50 copies each, they result in the sale of five time as many books as the blockbusters (these figures, which I have adapted from those reported by Anderson, are not far from the real figures for 2004). According to the Wikipedia page on *The Long Tail*, "a large proportion of Amazon.com's book sales come from obscure books that [are] not available from brick-and-mortar stores".

What this means is that your ideas can reach their audience. Social media and web sites like goodreads.com make possible a digital version of the book culture that used to revolve around printed books.

I just have to get used to reading eBooks. Perhaps the mini-iPad or the iPad-air will be good enough. For now, I have a paper-white Kindle and will try to get along with it![1]

---

[1] Almost eleven years after writing this article, I still haven't learned to take pleasure in reading eBooks...

The World as I see it

Originally posted in my blog on 2014-08-17.

Published with minor modifications by the ACT Writers Centre on 2014-11-06.

HISTORY

The World as I see it

The Path to Terrorism

I know that physically we are almost identical to the savages that 70,000 year ago left Africa to populate the world. But I am always amazed to discover how senselessly violent modern humans still can be. On an evolutionary scale, seventy millennia are a comparatively short period of time. Therefore, it is no surprise that our emotions and impulses haven't changed. But shouldn't we have learned to control them?

I am not talking about the Vulcan[1] discipline that can completely suppress emotions. It would be enough if we managed to avoid domestic and sectarian violence.

For most of our existence, human males needed aggressiveness to survive in a hostile and wild world but, in our modern society, testosterone-driven violence is a hindrance to true civilisation. Nothing is completely good or completely bad, and without ambition and stamina we would have failed to progress in many areas of human endeavour. Nevertheless, we shouldn't let our desire to assert ourselves lead us to hate and violence.

There is so much to say.

At the root of most acts of violence that we see reported in the daily news is a combination of desperation, intolerance, and greed.

This certainly applies to terrorism. I don't condone for a moment the act of detonating a bomb in the midst of a peaceful crowd. I couldn't do it. And yet, I can understand why some decide to blow themselves up in a market square full of people. They are desperate. They are alienated and see

---

[1] https://philosophynow.org/issues/106/Star_Treks_Stoics_The_Vulcans

no peaceful means to achieving the society they are striving for.

Being born is a lottery: you can hit the jackpot and enter the world in a developed country like Australia, Europe, or North America; or you can draw a blank and come to life in places like Gaza, Rwanda, or Somalia.

Those who like me were born in a western developed country are among the lucky ones. It is therefore up to us to reach out to the less fortunate ones. Ours is the greatest responsibility. If we don't manage to foster tolerance and understanding, how can we expect the dispossessed to do it?

Imagine to be a palestinian young man. You were born in a refugee camp in Jordan and grew up in a shack made of cardboard and corrugated iron. During the day, the temperature under the metal roof reached fifty degrees centigrades. You and your four siblings shared two cots, until you grew out of them and had to sleep on the ground. An open sewer ran on the back. In Summer, the stench was almost intolerable, and in Winter, when the occasional rains fell, a brown smelly liquid seeped under the back wall into your living area.

When you were seven, your little sister Jamila fell ill. She had a diarrhoea that didn't want to stop. Your mother took her to the dispensary and you went along. It was a big hut painted white with a red crescent moon and a red cross above the door. A pale doctor in a splattered white coat and a funny accent gave to your mother some pills for Jamila. Fortunately, a couple of days later, everything was back to normal.

When you reached ten years of age, you were given the daily chore to go to the well and fetch water. You had to queue up sometimes for half an hour before reaching the pump, and then drag back home the plastic tank with twenty litres of water. It was heavy, and you had to stop several times and take a rest. Your father had managed to find a job in Amman as a construction labourer, but it was poorly paid, and barely enough to feed a family of seven.

One day, your father managed to hook up your home to electricity and bought a second-hand TV set. The TV programmes made you realise that not everybody was living like you. Some people had beautiful houses with swimming pools and gleaming cars. Some people wore immaculate clothes and shining shoes.

At the koranic school, older boys told you that you were living in the dusty camp because the Israelis had thrown your family out of your own country. You learned that you couldn't ever hope of doing most of what you saw people on TV do. You learned that you were stuck where you were, without hope of ever improving your condition.

Some of your teenager friends got involved in minor crimes. A camera snatched from the shoulder of a fat tourist, sun glasses taken from a car left open, a case of bottles stolen from the back of a truck. You didn't want to go down that path. You wanted to do the right thing, but there was nothing to do. In part to combat boredom, you started going every day to a mosque with an energetic and young imam. His speeches touched your heart. They encouraged you to take pride in your faith. Judaism and Christianity were stepping stones leading to the only true religion: Islam.

Slowly slowly, you began seeing yourself as an island of integrity in a world that was disintegrating around you. You took distance from your friends and their petty thefts. You rejected the luxuries you saw on TV as the manifestation of moral decadence. You assiduously studied the Koran and felt that your faith was growing stronger.

One day, the imam introduced you to a young man. He spoke with an accent you hadn't heard before. You later learned that it was from Saudi Arabia. He asked you whether you wanted to do something for your People, and you replied yes, without hesitation. He took a picture of you with a small camera and said that you would hear from him again. One month later, you were on a non-stop flight from Amman to Karachi. In your shirt pocket you had a Syrian passport with a name that was not yours. You were excited. Finally, you would be doing something to fight against the infidels who had stolen your land and subdued your nation.

From Karachi you flew to Islamabad, and from there you travelled on a truck across the border with Afghanistan. During the next two weeks, in a training camp fifty kilometres East of Jalalabad, you learned how to fight, how to build pipe bombs, and, most importantly, that there were many other young men who thought like you. You felt part of the elite of pure warriors who would defeat the decadent infidels. You no longer needed to murmur your beliefs. Now you could shout them from the bottom of your heart and other would join you. It was glorious. There, among foreign mountains, you found yourself.

Your enthusiasm was misdirected. You were only trying to give a sense to a life devoid of any hope, and grabbed the first hand stretched towards you. In your thirst for a purpose, you lost contact with reality. You fell pray of people who had lost their way as well. How could you think that true Islam could sanction the senseless murder of innocent women and children? Unfortunately, there was nobody who could make you see how wrong you were.

If you think that the hypothetical character I just talked about is far fetched, think again. Peer pressure can push us towards ideas and actions that we wouldn't normally consider. And peer pressure combined with a feeling of powerlessness is what drives the desperate acts of violence we see every day on the news.

The World as I see it

In the mid seventies, while I was living in Rome, I shared an apartment with a friend of mine. One of her friends was a militant member of the university students' movement. For the sake of this narration, I will call him Marco, although he had in reality a different name. The movement sympathised with the extreme left of the political spectrum and Marco took part to many demonstrations against conservative policies. One day, he came to visit us after a demonstration. He was all excited and told us that he had thrown his first Molotov cocktail against the Police. These were times when the Red Brigades killed Aldo Moro, a Christian Democratic politician who had been Italy's prime minister.

We told Marco that he should have never done it, that police officers were only young men doing their job, that there was no civil war in Italy and no cause for starting one. I don't know whether he did it again and what happened to him, but his behaviour was emblematic of how left-oriented youth felt then. Why did he ignite a bottle half full of petrol and throw it at the Police? He felt that we were living in a police state, where civil liberties were being suppressed. He talked with people who reinforced his feelings and moved in a milieu where the government was the enemy. When the police charged and somebody put in his hand a Molotov cocktail, he had to throw it. He simply had to.

I know, detonating an explosive belt is much more serious than throwing an incendiary bottle, but the mechanisms behind them are the same. People become fanatics and terrorists step by step, when they see no way out of their situation. We have to understand and accept that these people are still human being, even if they treat their fellow humans with contempt.

The only way to eliminate terrorism is to remove the causes of desperation that afflict so many young men (and, increasingly, women) in our world. And, as I said, the initiative must come from us, the fat cats.

Originally posted in my blog on 2010-07-10.

Prohibition

This article is about the prohibition of drugs, but I will tackle that subject by talking about alcohol prohibition first. wiki.answers.com[1] reports that alcohol causes 100,000 deaths worldwide every year. I believe them. But then, why don't we do something about it? Should we ban alcohol? NO, WE SHOULDN'T because history has shown that ethanol prohibition doesn't work.

When the United States outlawed manufacture, sale, and transportation of alcohol between 1920 and 1933, they thought they were doing the right thing. They had to amend their constitution (the 18th amendment) because as a common law the ban would have been unconstitutional, and they were so convinced about it, that the House of Representatives approved the amendment with a bi-partisan majority of 282 against 128. The majority in the Senate was even greater, with 47 votes in favour and 8 against. It then took them longer than a decade to realise that it had been a bad decision. To their credit, the 21st amendment that repealed prohibition was passed in both the House of Reps and in the Senate with comfortable majorities.

Alcohol prohibition didn't work because, ultimately, people didn't want to give up their drinks. Humanity had been brewing beer for some 11,000 years, and producing wine for perhaps 8,000. In hindsight, the idea that any government could wean people from alcohol by decree was preposterous. At the beginning of prohibition, Reverend Billy Sunday said: "The reign of tears is over. The slums will soon be a memory. We will turn our prisons into factories and our jails into storehouses and corncribs. Men will walk upright now,

---

[1] http://wiki.answers.com/Q/
How_many_alcohol_related_deaths_occur_each_year

women will smile and children will laugh. Hell will be forever for rent".

It didn't work that way. In fact, prohibition was an important factor in the rise of organised crime in the U.S. I saw on the Web many statistics showing how crime increased during the prohibition years, but on the basis of those data we cannot determine what fraction of criminal acts was due to prohibition and what not. Crime might have increased at the same rate without prohibition.

I did find some plots that only relate to the prohibition laws[1]. Their author claims that the data originate from the U.S. Treasury Department, Bureau of Industrial Alcohol. Here is the first one, showing the number of convictions and acquittals:

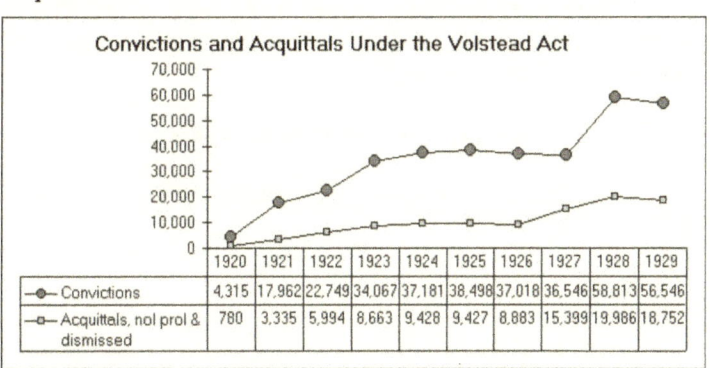

	1920	1921	1922	1923	1924	1925	1926	1927	1928	1929
Convictions	4,315	17,962	22,749	34,067	37,181	38,498	37,018	36,546	58,813	56,546
Acquittals, nol prol & dismissed	780	3,335	5,994	8,663	9,428	9,427	8,883	15,399	19,986	18,752

It shows that between 1920 and 1930, 444,342 people were prosecuted and 343,695 of them were convicted for producing, transporting, or consuming alcoholic beverages. But look at the steep increase. It means that the police and the courts were losing the "war on alcohol".

The second plot I want to show you is the number of police officers killed or injured while enforcing prohibition:

---
[1] http://www.druglibrary.org/prohibitionresults3.htm

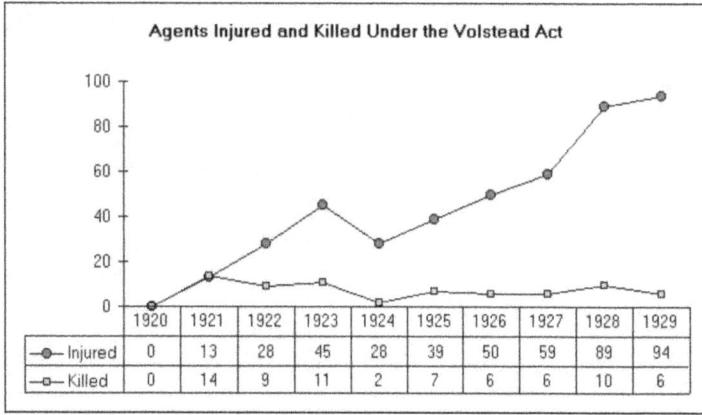

You might think that 71 police killed and 445 injured in ten years is not too bad, but they didn't need to occur. And look again at the steep increase. It was a real war, a fact that is confirmed by the third (and last) plot, showing the number of casualties per 1,000 arrests:

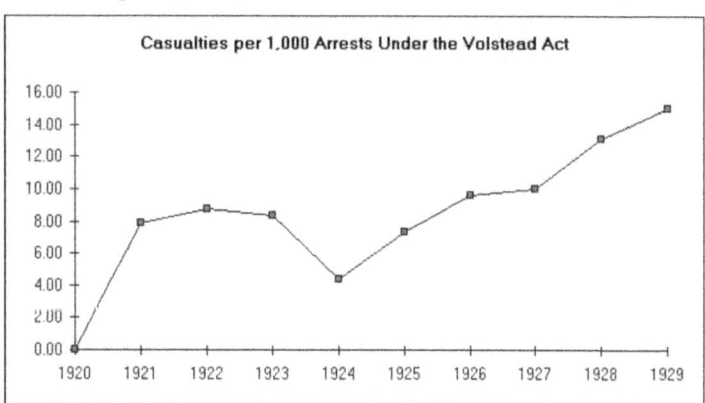

It proves that the arrests became increasingly violent. It was an escalating conflict.

The government wanted to force down the throat (pun intended :-) of the Americans a law that many American didn't want, and an increasing number of people broke it. I am sure that during those years the incidence of cirrhosis of the liver and cardiovascular diseases was reduced, but was it worth? I don't think so.

In the early 20th century, alcohol was also banned in Norway and Finland, but prohibition failed there as well.

As history has told us that the banning of alcohol is not a solution, to reduce the carnage on our roads caused by drunk drivers, we have introduced laws that limit what people are allowed to do while under the influence of alcohol. In this way, police and the judiciary protect the general population from violent or uncontrolled actions of individuals, rather than unnecessarily criminalise people as with the prohibitionist approach.

We have the same attitude towards tobacco. People can smoke it, but not when and where it can affect others. The laws don't prevent people from smoking. They only protect the rest of the community from the actions of the smokers.

SO, WHY ON EARTH DO WE KEEP WAGING THE SO-CALLED WAR ON DRUGS?

Because of the same misplaced moralistic attitude that led to the prohibition of alcohol in the U.S. That's why.

We all know that the cost of the war on drugs is exploding. I will just report some facts I found on the Web[1]. Between the years 1980 and 2000, the U.S. state and federal governments increased their spending on the drug war from a fistful of billions to forty billions; in 2002, the U.S. incarcerated almost as many people for breaking a drug law as it incarcerated in 1980 for all offences. Between 1990 and 1999, drug offences represented a 20% increase in the total growth of sentenced

---

1 The site was http://www.drugpolicy.org/ but the page I read in 2010 is no longer available.

prisoners under State jurisdiction. During that same time period, drug offenders were responsible for 60.9% of the federal prison population growth.

These trends mirror the trends of alcohol prohibition. We are all losing our world war on drugs as the U.S. lost their American war on alcohol in the 1920s. It is unequivocal. This drug prohibition is also responsible for an increased spreading of HIV infection due to needle sharing, all deaths by overdose, police corruption, deaths caused by turf wars between drug lords, and the list could continue.

There is only one solution: decriminalise drugs. Better: legalise them. All of them: opiates and cocaine, cannabis and LSD, ecstasy and amphetamines. Let people buy them from a chemist without a prescription. At the same time, introduce laws limiting what people can do under the influence of drugs and develop quick and easy to use devices to measure the amount of drugs that people have in their blood stream. The legalisation of drugs would pull the rug from under the feet of the drug barons. All the money that we now throw into the bottomless pit of the war on drugs would become available for more constructive purposes. And the nation would benefit from cocaine and heroine taxes as they now benefit from alcohol and tobacco taxes.

The critics of legalisation reason that more people would use drugs. Probably, but I contend that on the whole we would live in a better and safer society. Many people already consume drugs. Use the police to enforce legal limits of all dangerous substances when driving, rather than to chase people with a gram or two of marihuana in their pocket.

Originally posted in my blog on 2010-07-12.

The World as I see it

The World as I see it

The Manifesto of Fascist Racism

While researching for the historical novel I am writing, I stumbled onto the so called "Manifesto of Race", signed by ten Italian scientists and published in the magazine *La difesa della razza* ("The Defence of the Race") on August 5, 1938. It provides a glimpse into the Fascist ideology concerning an area that, I believe, is poorly known. Somehow, I feel compelled to translate the document into English for those who don't understand Italian.

Many personalities approved of the document when it was published, including, interestingly, Amintore Fanfani, who after the end of WWII became one of the most prominent members of the Democrazia Cristiana party and served as the Italian prime minister in five occasions.

Please don't blame me for the convoluted language. I did my best to preserve the style of the original text. I had to read some of the passages several times before making any sense of them.

Here it goes.

The Minister Secretary of the Party received on July 26 XVI a group of fascist scholars, professors in Italian universities, who, under the aegis of the Ministry of Popular Culture, edited or acceded to the propositions that lay the foundations of the fascist racism.

1. *HUMAN RACES DO EXIST. The existence of human races is not at all an abstraction of our spirit, but corresponds to a reality based on phenomena, which is material, and which can be perceived through our senses. This reality is represented by masses, almost always consisting of imposing numbers of millions of men with similar physical and psychological characteristics that were inherited and continue to be inherited. To say that*

there are human races does not necessarily mean that there are human races superior or inferior, but only that there are different human races.

2. *THERE EXIST LARGE RACES AND SMALL RACES. We must not only admit that there are major systematic groups, which are commonly called races, identified only through some characters, but we must also admit that there exist minor systematic groups (e.g., Northerners, the Mediterranean, etc.) identified by a greater number of common characteristics. These groups are, from a biological standpoint, the real races, the existence of which is an obvious truth.*

3. *THE CONCEPT OF RACE IS PURELY BIOLOGICAL. It is therefore based on considerations other than the concepts of people and nation, which are essentially founded on historical, linguistic, and religious considerations. But underlying the differences in peoples and nations are the differences of race. If the Italians are different from the French, Germans, Turks, Greeks, etc., it is not only because they have a different language and a different history, but because the racial constitution of these peoples is different. Since very ancient times, different proportions of different races have resulted in different peoples, regardless of whether one race has the absolute domination over all others, all races are harmoniously blended, or the races remain isolated from each other.*

4. *THE CURRENT POPULATION OF ITALY IS IN MAJORITY OF ARYAN ORIGIN, AND ITS CIVILISATION IS ARYAN. This population of Aryan civilisation has lived for several millennia in our country; very little is left of the civilisations of pre-Aryan peoples. The origin of the current Italians essentially comes from*

those same races that form and formed the forever-living fabric of Europe.

5. *THE ARRIVAL OF LARGE MASSES OF MEN IN HISTORICAL TIMES IS A LEGEND. After the invasion of the Longobards in Italy there were no other significant movements of people able to influence the racial aspect of the nation. It follows that, while in other European nations the racial composition has changed considerably even in modern times, in Italy, in broad terms, the racial composition of today is the same as that of a thousand years ago: the absolute majority of today's forty-four million Italians belongs therefore to families who have lived in Italy for at least a millennium.*

6. *BY NOW THERE EXISTS A PURE "ITALIAN RACE". This statement is not based on the confusion of the biological concept of race with the historical-linguistic concept of people and nation, but on the pure blood relationship that unites the today's Italians to the generations that for centuries have populated Italy. This ancient purity of blood is the greatest title of nobility of the Italian nation.*

7. *IT IS TIME THAT THE ITALIANS FRANKLY PROCLAIM THEMSELVES AS RACISTS. All the deeds that the Regime has so far accomplished in Italy are in essence racism. In the speeches of the Chief the recall to racial concepts has always been very frequent. The issue of racism in Italy must be dealt with from a purely biological point of view, with no philosophical or religious intentions. The concept of racism in Italy must be essentially Italian and its direction Aryan-Nordic. This does not mean, however, introducing in Italy the theories of German racism as they are or stating that the Italians and the Scandinavians are the same thing. Its purpose is only to point out to the Italians a physical and above all*

psychological model of human race that because of its purely European character, completely detaches itself from all extra-European races. It means elevating the Italian to an ideal of a higher consciousness of himself and of greater responsibility.

8. *IT IS NECESSARY TO MAKE A CLEAR DISTINCTION BETWEEN THE MEDITERRANEANS OF EUROPE (WESTERNERS) AND THE ORIENTALS AND AFRICANS. We have therefore to regard as dangerous the theories that support the African origin of some European peoples and incorporate in a common Mediterranean race Semitic and Hamitic populations by establishing relationships and ideological sympathies which are absolutely unacceptable.*

9. *JEWS DO NOT BELONG TO THE ITALIAN RACE. Nothing is in general left of the Semites that over the centuries have landed on the sacred soil of our fatherland. Even the Arab occupation of Sicily has left nothing behind, except the memory of some names; and in any case the process of assimilation was always very quick in Italy. The Jews are the only people that was never assimilated in Italy because it consists of non-European racial elements, absolutely different from the elements that gave rise to the Italians.*

10. *THE PURELY EUROPEAN PHYSICAL AND PHYCHOLOGICAL CHARACTER OF THE ITALIANS MUST NOT BE ALTERED IN ANY WAY. Marriage is permissible only within the European races, in which case one should not speak of true hybridism, as these races belong to a common strain and only differ in some characteristics, while being identical in many other. The purely European character of the Italians is altered from the crossing with any extra-European race, bearer of a*

civilisation different from the ancient civilisation of the Aryans.

The signatories were:

- Lino Businco, Assistant Lecturer in General Pathology, University of Rome
- Lidio Cipriani, Lecturer of Anthropology, University of Florence
- Arturo Donaggio, Director of the Neuropsychiatric Clinic, University of Bologna, and President of the Italian Society of Psychiatry
- Leone Franzi, Assistant in the Pediatric Clinic, University of Milan
- Guido Landra, Assistant Lecturer in Anthropology, University of Rome
- Nicola Pende, Director of the Institute of Special Medical Pathology, University of Rome
- Marcello Ricci, Assistant Lecturer in Zoology, University of Rome
- Franco Savorgnan, Professor of Demography, University of Rome, and President of the Central Institute of Statistics
- Sabato Visco, Director of the Institute of General Physiology, University of Rome, and Director of the National Institute of Biology, National Research Council
- Edoardo Zavattari, Director of the Institute of Zoology, University of Rome

Amazing. I find the sentence "It is time that the Italian frankly proclaim themselves as racist" particularly appalling. The Rome-Berlin Axis was a military coalition formed in October 1936. In 1938, Germany annexed Austria and started occupying Czechoslovakia. Mussolini wanted to ride the coat tails of the apparently unstoppable Nazi Germany. It is therefore not surprising that he introduced racial laws that would please Hitler.

Originally posted in my blog on 2010-10-12.

The World as I see it

Living in Italy during the Years of Lead

This article is about what happened to me one early morning of 1977.

At the time, I was sharing a large rented apartment with three friends: Bruna, Maia, and Annamaria. In case you are wondering, yes, they were three young ladies. The apartment was in Parioli, a rich quarter of Rome, and included four bedrooms, an eat-in kitchen, and a large hallway that functioned as a shared space.

We were all in our twenties and, as you can imagine, we often had lots of visitors, some of whom, not infrequently, stayed for the night and shared the bed with one [or more] of the permanent residents. It was a bit like a family and Bruna and I, being the eldest and the only ones in employment, assumed sometimes the role of the parents, although, truth be told, no one was interested in making it a permanent feature of our little community.

But I am digressing.

The evening before that fateful day, with what turned out to be a lucky break, we had not had received any visitors. So, as it was, there was only the four of us sleeping in the apartment, each one bravely alone in his or her bed.

At around four o'clock in the morning, I was woken up by Bruna with: "Giulio, Giulio, the police is here! Wake up!"

Summer nights in Rome can be quite warm, and I had taken up the habit of sleeping naked. From Bruna's tone, I had had the impression that she had not yet opened the entrance door. As a result of that assumption, as soon as I woke up, I became concerned that the police might knock it down. I jumped off the bed, grabbed my Vietnamese kimono from the back of a chair, and rushed out of my room.

You can imagine my surprise when I discovered that a dozen police officers, some in uniform and some in civilian clothes, were already standing in the hallway. I found myself surrounded by stern-looking men in my [perhaps-not-so-glorious] nakedness, holding in my right hand a white kimono with a black floral design. I recovered quickly and, after mumbling something like "just a second, please," turned my back to them and returned to my room, where I put my kimono on in privacy.

The police scrambled through all the rooms and collected a series of items that they considered suspicious. Among them were a small wooden pipe, the couple of spent cartridges of the high-speed automatic rifle I had kept as a memento from my time in the military officers' school, and some cinnamon sticks bound together with a stripe of maize husk. No cannabis or hashish, which, at the time, was actually quite surprising. They put everything into a cardboard box and took us to the police station.

The three officers that squeezed with me into the lift couldn't refrain from commenting on my uninhibited little community. They found it particularly interesting that I was the only male and didn't doubt for a second that my three friends were in fact nothing else than my private harem. I said: "they are just friends," but that didn't manage to wipe off their faces the grins of 'I know better than that, you sultan'. In a sense their opinion suited me fine because they would then treat me with more respect, and when you find yourself at the receiving end of a police action, everything helps.

Anyhow, at the police station we were told to sit on four chairs in a room in which the only other pieces of furniture were a desk and a chair with an officer sitting on it. Somebody came to take Maia to another room and the other three of us began speculating on what was going on. We were in the middle of the so-called Years of Lead, dominated by fear of the Red Brigates and their actions. Therefore, the first thing we thought was that our arrest had to do with it, although we knew we had not done anything that could even remotely be associated with terrorism.

Potere Operaio (Workman's Power) and *Lotta Continua* (Sustained Struggle), two extreme-left movements that had been going strongly in the early seventies, had been recently shut down, and some of the leaders of the Red Brigades had been arrested a couple of years earlier. But the climate of terror would continue for years. Less than a year after the events I am describing, the horror of terrorism in Italy would peak with the murdering of the prominent Italian politician Aldo Moro.

The officer sitting behind the desk must have felt disturbed by our chatting because he raised his eyes from the newspaper and barked: "Shut up!" We decided that it was prudent to comply. If you haven't experienced it, you have no idea how different the world looks when the police have you in their sight...

After at least a couple of hours, the mystery of our arrest was revealed. I had been suspected to be the leader of an extreme-left terrorist cell. Those days, some young professionals with an irreprehensible curriculum sometimes devoted some of their money and time to topple the established political system. Such small cells operated almost independently from each other. Therefore, it was a tedious and unrewarding job to root them out one by one. I fitted the profile beautifully.

Some time before the events I am narrating, Maia had met on a bus an old friend from her same region of Sardinia. After a chat and promises to meet again, she had given him our telephone number. That fellow, as it turned out, had been (or was later; I am not sure) involved in acts of terrorism and even killed a *carabiniere* in a shootout. When the police finally arrested him, they found in his pocket a booklet with many contacts, including Maia's (i.e., mine).

Fortunately, Maia managed to convince the police that she had not had any further contact with her terrorist acquaintance and that she, in any case, didn't share his views. To be honest, I am not sure whether she told the whole truth and nothing but the truth, so help her God, but that is now immaterial. It also helped to exonerate us that at the time I was an army commissioned officer of the reserve and the son of a decorated police officer.

The lieutenant who gave me back the cardboard box with our stuff was even a bit apologetic. Not apologetic enough to drive us back home, though. When I arrived home, I noticed that my spent rifle cartridges had not been returned to me. Of course, I thought, civilians are not allowed to keep anything that has to do with military weapons and ammunitions. But I was a bit annoyed. What damage to the state could I have possibly caused with a couple of spent 7.62mm NATO cartridges?

But the law is the law. Isn't it?

Originally posted in my blog on 2010-10-31.

The World as I see it

End-of-Year Cleanup

I should have published this story on January 1st, but better late than never.

As you perhaps know, I grew up in Rome (Italy). On the last day of each year, the busses stopped running a few hours before midnight and retreated to their depots. But it wasn't simply to give to drivers and conductors the opportunity to celebrate the coming of the new year with their families. It was to ensure their safety.

Yes. Their safety because when I was a boy, it was a Roman tradition to dispose of unwanted stuff by throwing it out of the window. Literally.

Why bring junk to the tip when you can simply throw it out? Besides being simpler and more economical, at a time when the majority of people could not afford to buy a car, it was fun!

Can you imagine the impact of an old easy chair when it hits the sidewalk after a "flight" from the fourth or the sixth floor?

You could throw out everything, including old sinks and toilet bowls, with seat and all. A walk in the early hours of the new year, before the teams of garbage collectors started the thankless task of cleaning up the streets, was a unique experience. In some quarters you literally had to walk in the middle of the street in order to negotiate your way through. At least, with all the broken glass and empty cans littering the streets, there was no chance that a car would be around to hit you.

I lived with my parents, sister, and grandmother, on the third floor of Via Alessandria 119, just outside the high wall that the Romans built around the city some two thousand years ago. It was quite central, and very near the place where the troops of the Kingdom of Italy breached the wall on 20 September 1870 to "liberate" Rome from the Vatican.

Anyhow, you can see below a snapshot of the street "borrowed" from Google's street view. You can see the entrance door and the windows.

From one of those windows, my family and I enjoyed the view of the "new-year dumping" and, sometimes, threw something away ourselves, although I don't remember that we ever got rid of very bulky items.

One year, when I was between four and seven years old, we had a carton of persimmons who had become a bit too ripe. Who knows why we had it, but I remember that at midnight of December 31st we used them to bombard a car that somebody, very imprudently, had left parked on the other side of our street. The fruits were very soft, and I am sure that we didn't do any damage to the car, but I can only imagine what its owner must have thought when he saw it completely covered by a orangey sticky goo.

I wouldn't do it now, and I cannot imagine (but don't know it) that Romans still throw rubbish out of the window on the last night of the year. Still, at a time when very few families had a TV set or money to spend on fireworks, it was of great entertainment.

Italy is much more civilised these days...

Originally posted in my blog on 2012-01-08.

The World as I see it

Soldiers and Dismembered Bodies. What else is New?

The publication of photos that show US soldiers posing with dismembered suicide bombers have drawn almost universal condemnation.

I confess I don't understand what the fuss is all about. Perhaps we have become accustomed to neat pictures of laser-guided missiles hitting their targets with uncanny precision, and have forgotten that war on the ground is not like that.

Although I know that sometimes wars are unavoidable and even appropriate, I am at heart a pacifist and a non-violent. To the point that I avoid swatting flies. That said, the images of soldiers pissing on dead enemies or posing with dead bodies, dismembered or not, don't surprise me in the least.

I would never do it, but then, I am not a soldier fighting a guerrilla war. To kill other human beings is not part of human nature. For the vast majority of people, killing somebody is a shock. Even when the killing is done in self defence. That's why combat training always involves creating automatisms and dehumanising the enemy. The more a soldier sees an enemy as a target or a threat rather than as a fellow human being, the more he is likely to shoot first and survive.

And then, there is the suppressed fear of dying and suffering, which bottles up on every mission and sortie. It is inevitable that under such circumstances, some soldiers go further than what we, watching a sanitised war on TV from our comfortable sofa, find acceptable.

The massacres of My Lai and Srebrenica are excesses that happened because the soldiers didn't consider their victims as other human beings. Same story with the Nazis and the

Holocaust: it was OK to kill the Jews because, according to Hitler & Co., they were subhuman.

Politicians want to have the cake and eat it too. Fortunately, the soldier who made the photos public, reminded us that war is not nice. The only clean war is a war that doesn't take place at all!

Originally posted in my blog on 2012-04-21.

POLITICS

The World as I see it

Marriage for All

This article describes my position concerning same-sex marriages.

I expect that most people, with the exception of religious bigots, would support the formalisation of homosexual unions.

After all, it makes sense that if two people form a stable relationship and share their lives with one another, they should be able to care for each other, inherit from each other, and, in general, have their union formally recognised. And this, regardless of their political convictions, religious beliefs, ethnicity, sexual preferences, or gender.

Opponents of same-sex marriage, including many of our politicians, insist that the word "marriage" should be reserved for heterosexual couples. Further, they claim that in making that statement they are not guided by religious beliefs, but only by their personal moral rules.

I find such a position unreasonable. Some of those politicians, regardless of their denials, do it because of their religious affiliation. Others probably believe that the country is not ready for same-sex marriage and don't want to jeopardise they possibilities of re-election.

I see marriage as a contract between two people. Why somebody should be excluded from it is for me a totally alien concept. There was a time when so-called "inter-racial" marriages were illegal. Worse than that, there are still countries where two people cannot marry if they belong to different religions. In our "enlightened" western civilisation, though, these are things of the past. The discrimination on the basis of gender will have to go as well.

The World as I see it

One of the apparently reasonable objections to gay marriages is that if marriage were open to same-sex couples, they would then be able to adopt children. The objection is that a child, to grow into a balanced member of society, needs both a father figure and a mother figure. There might be some truth in such an opinion, but who is to say that two men or two women couldn't assume the diversity of roles that a child need? I would go even further and claim that the two members of a couple always have different roles within their relationship, whether they share the same gender or not.

Besides, a growing portion of marriages ends up in divorce, which indicates that always more children live, at least for a while, in a dysfunctional or, at the very least, unhappy and unbalanced family. And the number of single parents is also on the rise. The fact that two people can biologically procreate has never been a guarantee that they will be good parents.

Further, a growing proportion of couples decide not to marry and prefer to live in a de-facto relationship. So much so, that laws have been created to recognise such informal unions. So, why should it be possible for heterosexual couples to form "loose" unions but not for homosexual couple to form "tight" unions?

I tell you, in fewer years that you can count on the fingers of one hand, gay marriage will be accepted in many, if not most, western countries[1].

Actually, why limit the number of people who can get married to two? If marriage is really to be seen as a civil contract between adults, perhaps it would make sense to extend it to more that two people, all bound by the same rules. I know, I am being provocative and perhaps, on closer examination, there are many reason for limiting marriage contracts to two

---

1 Indeed!

people. But the point I am trying to make is that people still attach to marriage law a special status that it shouldn't have.

Part of the problem is that we use the same word for two completely different things: one is a religious ceremony celebrated by a cleric, and one is the stipulation of a contract regulated by the Marriage Act.

We should split the two as clearly as possible. I confess I don't know what the situation is in Australia, but in Italy, where I grew up, thanks to the Lateran Treaty of 1929 between the Catholic Church and Mussolini, priests can transfer catholic marriages to the civil authorities. No wonder that then people confuse the two.

Let the religious people have their marriages as they like, and everybody else, heterosexual or not, sign the contracts they want.

All those who oppose same-sex marriage claim that their objections have nothing to do with religion. This is obviously (at least to me) nonsensical. The fact is that marriage is still seen by many as a "holy matrimony", a union sealed by God.

For me, to limit marriage to people of opposite sexes is an act of discrimination, as absurd as if there were the requirement of a minimum difference in weight or age or colour of the skin.

In Australia, almost one third of people never marry and one third of marriages end up in divorce. Furthermore, there are more de-facto relationships than married couples. The idea that marriage is one of the pillars of our society is therefore a bit outdated.

A marriage is a contract. It spells out duties and rights like any other contract. As such, it should be accessible to everyone who accept some obligations in order to enter a recognised form of relationship.

The discrimination against same-sex marriages is a relic of the past that should be disposed of without so much fussing about. I understand the value of traditions, but marriage exclusively between a man and a woman should be confined to the history books exactly like the *ius primae noctis*.

Originally posted in my blog in two parts on 2010-11-22 and 2011-10-23.

Casualties

Another Australian soldier has died in Afghanistan. It saddens me to think that a hail of nails and ball bearings on a dusty road killed a young, strong, and courageous man. Like most people, I know what it means to lose somebody you care about, and my thoughts go to Sergeant Wood's wife.

Still, as sorry as I was to hear of Brett Wood's death, I was amazed to hear radio commentators ask whether the Australian presence in Afghanistan will be affected by it. At risk of appearing cynical, one more death doesn't change anything. I don't even understand why anybody would raise the issue at all. Of course the Australian policy concerning Afghanistan will not change. And rightly so. With a dangerous operation involving thousands of soldiers and civilians, we can be happy that only twenty-four have died. There will be more casualties. For sure.

Should we be in Afghanistan at all? I will answer with another question: if you saw a bully humiliate a weaker child on a schoolyard or a violent man assault a woman, should you intervene? To what extent do you try to reason with somebody who bases his existence on violence and abuse? It comes to a point where you cannot simply look on and enjoy your peaceful corner of the world.

I am not so naïve as to think that interventions in countries like Afghanistan and Libya are purely for humanitarian reasons. And the proof of that is that many/most/all governments have a history of supporting tyrants as long as their actions suit the perceived interests of their countries, like when the USA armed Saddam Hussein because he was at war with Iran.

Nevertheless, I think there would be less suffering in our world if the Taliban were prevented from practising their medieval beliefs.

To make another parallel, I don't like antibiotics and heavy drugs, but sometimes they are necessary. A healthy diet and some placebos like Homeopathic medicines and food supplements are not always enough. The Taliban and groups like Al Qaeda are like tumours and drug-resistant viruses. If what it takes to keep them in check is chemotherapy, then so be it.

And now that I have started with this tirade, I feel compelled to talk about Israel as well. No idea why. The Israelis think that the centuries of prosecution culminating with the Holocaust give them the right to do what they want. They reject criticism directed towards their policies by saying that it is a manifestation of anti-Semitism. And most governments let them get away with it for fear of upsetting significant parts of their electorates.

This is nonsense. Israel is an arrogant little state that has been oppressing the Palestinian people for decades. They feel threatened by the countries that surround them. I understand that. And we shouldn't forget the Holocaust. But it is time that we look at the Israeli for what they are and what they do right now, rather than feel sorry for what Hitler did to their grandparents.

Originally posted in my blog on 2011-05-24.

Checks on Senior Law-Enforcement Agents

Yesterday, I watched Four Corners, one of Australia's leading current affairs programs (without advertising), and feel compelled to reflect on it.

It was about Mark Standen[1], assistant director of the NSW Crime Commission or, to say it plainly, the top lawman in drug-laws enforcement of the most populous Australian state.

To summarise what happened, I will just copy a paragraph from Australian ABC's website: "On Thursday 11th August, after a five month trial, a jury found Mark Standen guilty of conspiring to import and supply 300 kilograms of pseudo-ephedrine, a chemical that could produce $60 million worth of 'ice', or crystal meth. He was also found guilty of perverting the course of justice."

After a thirty-year career in law enforcement, Standen let himself be corrupted. It probably didn't help that he had some gambling debts, but for me an important question is: how can an honest man get involved with crimes that literally contribute to killing young people?

My answer is that he must have had in himself enough selfishness to commit a crime regardless of the consequences.

Although obviously I cannot be sure, I don't think I could ever get involved with drug trafficking. Respect for other human being drives all my relationships, from the most fleeting to those that have remained with me for the largest part of my adult life.

What arrogance to think that, although you earn 250,000 AU$/year, you are justified in contributing to waste other

---

1 https://www.abc.net.au/4corners/standen-the-inside-man/2855724

people's lives to feed your gambling habits or to buy jewellery from Tiffany for your girlfriend.

We know that crooks can be everywhere. In a country like Australia, the vast majority of people at worst only indulge themselves in some tax cheating or driving above the speed limit. Not acceptable activities, for sure, although somehow tolerated by many. But drug trafficking is something else.

I don't think he became a criminal for some ten thousand dollars. As I said above, he must have held a seed of criminality inside himself well before the opportunity to smuggle synthetic-drug precursors presented itself.

Therefore, a key question for me is: how could such a latent criminal reach the top echelons of law enforcement?

Certainly, Standen must have gone through several levels of vetting checks, specifically designed to weed out potential crooks. And yet, he was clever enough to pass them all.

That's why I support the idea of instituting an independent commission of enquiry into his career in law enforcement.

We know that good networking is essential to progress within any organisation, and we also know that there is solidarity within the ranks of organisations that sometimes have to face popular criticism or opposition, like the armed forces, the fire brigades, the police, the judiciary, etc.

Still, to what scrutiny was Standen subjected before and after reaching senior positions in the NSW Crime Authority? Was he checked at all once he became assistant director? Perhaps not. Perhaps it was thought that if he was there he must have been OK.

Standen's misdeed were only discovered because the Dutch police found out that an English "drug facilitator" (an interesting item to put on a CV!), was in contact with Bill

Jalalaty, an Australian businessman. When the Australian Federal Police, on request of the Dutch, placed Jalalaty's mobile phone under surveillance, they discovered that he was having suspicious conversations with none other than the top drug-cop of NSW.

Were Standen's gambling problems known within the Agency and, if yes, why wasn't he considered to be a risk?

A wide-scoped investigation should ascertain whether the vetting process applied within law-enforcement agencies, especially concerning seniors officials, is sound. Perhaps they are, and Standen was only an exceptional deceiver who managed to slip through the net. An almost-impossible feat never to be repeated for decades to come.

But perhaps the vetting process has shortcomings that should be fixed.

I believe that there should be regular checks on the presence of risk factors, like gambling, medication, and drinking problems. And not only on the subject, but also on his immediate family. I know: right to privacy and all that... But if you want to be a commissioner in a crime authority, you should be prepared to forfeit some of those rights.

There are jobs in law enforcement and intelligence that are too sensitive to be left in the hands of potential crooks. Any risk factor should be carefully considered.

Some criminal will always manage to escape detection. Ultimately, it is the prevailing culture of a nation that determines whether the authorities are honest or not. But checks are better than trust, when so much is at stake.

Originally posted in my blog on 2011-08-16.

The World as I see it

The World as I see it
Multiculturalism and Religion

I just read a couple of articles on the Canberra Times, Canberra's major daily newspaper, that made me reflect on some issues connected with religion and multiculturalism.

First of all, I discovered that in the Australian Federal Parliament, before each sitting day, the Speaker of the House and the President of the Senate request God's blessing and read the Lord's prayer.

Apparently, the political leaders agree that this 'monocultural' and discriminating practice should continue. I personally, perhaps not surprising to those who know me even just a bit, find it appalling.

Although Australia doesn't have a state religion like Britain and the Australian constitution even prohibits the establishment of a national church, we don't have a clear separation of State and Church.

One side effect of this is that we spend a lot of money to support religious schools. I agree that in a free country religious organisations should be able to indoctrinate (ahem... I meant: to educate ;-) children in the tenets of their religion. But what I don't agree about is that they receive state subsidies to do it.

In general, the existence of expensive private schools encourages and perpetuates a classist society. Therefore, I am against public funding of private schools, whether they are religious or not. The objection that abolition of public funding would force closure of many private schools is not a valid one because it has been shown over and over again that government subsidies of private enterprises result in inefficiency and complacency. That money should go to improve public schools: higher pay for teachers, smaller classes, better infrastructures. Then, with time, the idea that private schools provide better education would fade away.

But I am digressing...

By funding religious schools, besides diverting money away from public schools, the State legitimises them. I don't think that any public penny should support, for example, the juxtaposition on equal footing of unprovable beliefs and proven scientific theories, like stating that Intelligent Design is as valid a theory as Evolution by Natural Selection.

About Multiculturalism, I would like first of all to state unequivocally that I am in favour of maintaining cultural diversity. I read in several articles that Multiculturalism in Europe has failed. This might well be, and I cannot be sure that the idea of Multiculturalism is in fact workable on the long run. But it seems to me that we have no choice, and that we should work hard to keep it alive.

What are the alternatives? Ghettoes? A revival of the White-Australia Policy? Forcible integration by banning cultural diversity? I don't think so.

In Australia, despite some cases of ghettoisation, like with the Vietnamese community in Cabramatta in the late 20th century, Multiculturalism seems to be working. I feel I don't need to cease being an Italian and a Roman in order to be and Australian and a Canberran.

This is what I understand as Multiculturalism: a blending of communities that integrate their traditions into the fabric of Australian society. I have no doubt that Australia has benefited from the presence of substantial minorities coming from different cultures and languages.

Perhaps, if my skin were not lily-white, I would feel differently. Perhaps, if I had not been educated in a European country, I would find it much more difficult to integrate into the Australian society while maintaining what makes me an Italian. Perhaps, if I were a Muslim man and wore a black long beard, I would be looked at with hostility and fear. I don't know. I hope not.

I believe that everybody should be able to maintain their traditions and, even if I am an atheist, practice their faiths. But, although I am not in favour of a policy of total assimilation, there are practices that I don't find acceptable. I know: who am I to claim the higher moral ground? Why should the rules of our society, based on the Christian tradition and an Anglo-Saxon model of state, be better or preferable to those of other societies?

These are not easy issues to talk about, but they have to be resolved nonetheless, if we want to maintain a peaceful coexistence in our country.

I am against forced marriages, infibulation of women, circumcision of women and men, and violent domination of female family members, to name some. Also, I find that punishing people by stoning to death or by cutting a limb has no place in a modern society. Therefore, I would never agree to introduce a form of Sharia law as, I believe, has happened in Britain. The laws of the country should equally apply to everyone.

Circumcision of minors, unless done for documented and validated medical reasons, is nothing else than gratuitous mutilation. I would like to see it banned in Australia. If Jews and Muslims, instead of cutting the foreskin of their male children, had the tradition of cutting off their left ear, I am confident that it would have been banned long ago. Then, why should religious circumcision be tolerated?

We now condemn how children were treated in Australian orphanages decades ago. They were subjected to damagingly harsh discipline and physically and sexually abused. We now condemn the practice of taking aboriginal children away from their families to educate them in our European ways. We now think that lashing people until their back is reduced to a bloody pulp is barbaric. We are appalled at learning that people were routinely lobotomised in order to calm them down. And yet, not long ago, these practices were perfectly acceptable.

Our society is based on respecting the integrity of the individuum, both physical and psychological. The general principle is that we are free to do what we want as long as we don't affect others. This is why we now ban smoking almost everywhere: to protect the health of those who would be passive smokers. But I find it absurd that we can tell a parent: stop smoking in the car if your child is on board, but please feel free to cut away a part of his body if it makes you feel better!

Is this arbitrary? Absolutely! And who should be entrusted with the task of deciding what is acceptable and what is not? In a democratic country, only one answer is possible: through legislation passed by elected representatives.

Inevitably, cultural minorities will invoke the application of anti-discrimination laws designed to protect them to continue practices that the vast majority of Australian people would find unacceptable. And so they should. But a culture that is unable to adapt is destined to oblivion. In the end, they should accept the changes, as we all do.

In my opinion, practices should be considered in terms of the permanent impact they have on the subject. One month after I was born, I was taken to a church and received some cold water sprinkled on my head. I cried for that, but no permanent damage was done. But if my father had come from some regions of Sudan, he would have made three cuts on my face, which would have scarred me for life. I say: if we have to allow people to scar their children in the name of traditions, to hell with those traditions!

Originally posted in my blog on 2012-03-13.

The World as I see it

Boat People

Every year, some thousand people are desperate enough to attempt the dangerous crossing from Indonesia to Australia on rickety boats. They pay thousands of dollars to the unscrupulous operators who own the boats, in the hope that they will be allowed to remain in Australia as refugees.

Most of them get recognition for their refugee status[1] and, slowly and painfully, find their place in our society.

Unfortunately, these people, who leave behind a life full of violence, abuse, and fear, have become a virtual ball that the two major Australian parties (Labour and Liberal) play to score political points.

In Australia, if you enter the country illegally (i.e., without a valid visa) and apply for refugee status, you are kept in detention until your application is processed. This would be acceptable if the processing took, say, one month. I am sure that everyone, after years of deprivation and a perilous journey, would be happy to relax for a short while in a comparatively comfortable place with plenty of food, clean water, and medical assistance. I know I would.

But the processing can take YEARS!

Often the problem is that the Australian Security Intelligence Organisation (ASIO) encounters difficulties in determining the identity of the applicants and in ensuring that they do not represent a threat to national security (i.e., that they are not terrorists or criminals in disguise). This is understandable, but what is wrong with letting them out, with some form of control, like regular reporting or perhaps, if you really are paranoid, GPS ankle-bands?

---

1 This is no longer the case, as people deemed to have entered Australia illegally are currently never allowed to settle.

As a result of this mandatory detention policy, families are split for years, and cases of self-arm and suicide are more frequent among detainees than in the rest of the population. What a shame, for such an affluent society. Besides, if these people were allowed to live a reasonably normal life and to look for work, besides being the humane thing to do, it couldn't possibly cost to the taxpayers more than maintaining detentions facilities scattered throughout the country[1].

According to both major parties and the Australian newspapers, the Australian public is very sensitive to the integrity of Australian borders. This might be true, but then, rather than encourage alarmism every time a boat is intercepted, they should point out that every year some fifty-thousand people fly into the country legally and then overstay their visas. It would take longer than a decade of boat people (estimated on the average of arrivals during the past 2.5 years) to make up the same number of travellers that in any single year overstay their visa.

These people who come by boat could have not even applied for a passport in their country. It is inhumane to lock them up as soon as they reach our shores. Who bloody cares about a couple of thousand people more or less? I say: let them in and treat them with dignity. Show them, the Australian public, and the world that we care. But perhaps we don't. Not enough.

Then there is the myth of deterrence. It was Paul Keating who, as a Labour Prime Minister, introduced the policy of "mandatory detention", to discourage people from coming by boat.

Then, John Howard, some years later, as a Liberal prime minister, introduced "offshore processing" for the same reason. Asylum seekers were transported to Manus Island in

---

[1] Or in some Pacific island.

Papua New Guinea and Nauru while their application was being processed. Also, towards the end of 1999, the Howard government introduced the Temporary Protection Visas (TPVs). Refugees were given a three-year visa rather than a permanent one.

The Liberals claim that their TPVs worked as a deterrent because the number of refugees trickled to almost nothing. It is true that in 1999 there were 3721 arrivals by boat and in 2002 only 1 (yes: a single person), but the arrivals in 2000 were 2939, and in 2001 the number of arrivals reached 5516![1]. If the TPVs had been effective, it would have not taken two years to see a reduction of arrivals.

The Liberals contradict themselves. They explain the 2849 arrivals of 2009 with the fact that the Labour prime minister Rudd abolished the TPVs in 2008. But then, why should it have take two years to see the opposite effect when the TPVs were introduced?

Some months ago, the current Labour government came up with the concept of "regional processing centres". They said: refugees are a regional issue, not just an Australian one. Therefore, we should set up regional centres where all refugees of the region can be processed. Very innovative (although not in agreement with the Geneva Convention). But East Timor didn't agree to take the centre.

The Liberals pushed for Nauru, whose government would have welcomed such a centre. But the government stated that Nauru was impossible because it was not a signatory of the Geneva Convention and they remained unmoved in their position when Nauru did sign the convention on refugees. It seems obvious to me that the government rejected the idea of

---

1 Found on a page of the Australian Parliament website that no longer exists.

a regional centre in Nauru because the Liberals had been pushing for it. That's all. The convention was just an excuse.

Things seemed to be moving ahead on the deterrence front when the Labour government of Julia Gillard signed an agreement with Malaysia (which, incidentally, is not a signatory of the convention, and apparently treats its refugees in an appalling way, with beatings and unjustified arrests). Australia would take from Malaysia four thousand recognised refugees and send there in exchange the first eight hundred boat people that would reach Australia after the signing the agreement.

It certainly would have been a deterrent for people to try to reach Australia by boat from Indonesia knowing that they would be immediately flown to Malaysia.

But somebody applied to the High Court of Australia on behalf of some of the people who were going to be deported to Malaysia to have the agreement reviewed, and the High Court ruled that it was in violation of Australia's international agreements and therefore illegal. In fact, it wrote such a ruling that all offshore processing became impossible.

The government formulated a law that would have allowed them to establish national policies in violation of international agreements, but the Greens, who support the current minority government, disagreed. They had always been in favour of onshore processing and didn't change their mind. And the Liberals were happy to score a political point against the government by opposing the law, despite the fact that they had invented offshore processing in 2001.

In any case, I question the morality of cajoling refugees so that they are dissuaded from coming. I don't find it acceptable to put under pressure people who are already so desperate.

Earlier today, I talked about this subject with my local member of parliament. He said that Labour's goal is to prevent people from taking such a desperate journey. Fair enough, but we are not responsible for them. We should work with the neighbouring countries and try to catch the criminals that cash on people's desperation, but once somebody decides to take the journey and arrives on our shores, we should treat them with compassion, not throw them into jail or fly them off to Malaysia...

Originally posted in my blog on 2011-10-22.

The World as I see it

Drug Scores

Here is an interesting diagram produced in 2010 by the UK Advisory Council for the Misuse of Drugs (I know, the text on the axes is a bit small...):

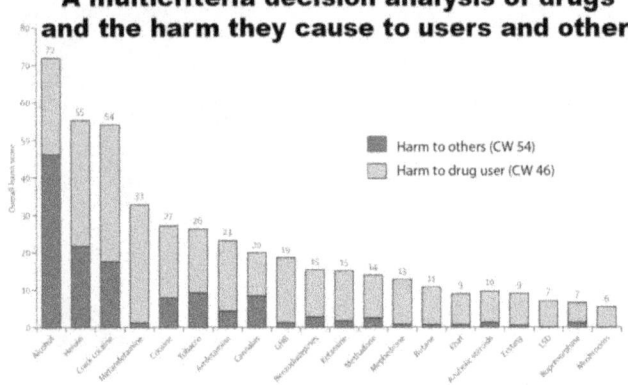

What interests me is the harm done to others. The seven most damaging drugs are (in decreasing order of harm caused): alcohol, heroin, crack cocaine, tobacco, cannabis, cocaine, and amphetamine.

Alcohol is more than twice as harmful to others than heroin, and tobacco is worse than cocaine, cannabis, and amphetamine.

And yet, while in most countries you can buy alcohol and tobacco in drugstores (interesting name for a type of shop, in this context), in many places you can end up in jail for smoking a joint. I might be mistaken but, as far as I know, except in Holland and California, you cannot even use cannabis for therapeutic purposes[1]. How ridiculous is that?

---

1 You can now use cannabis for medicinal purposes in Australia, although it isn't easy and it remains quite expensive.

The World as I see it

I am in favour of LEGALISING all drugs (not just decriminalising some of them).

I have heard lots of arguments and discussions concerning pros and cons, but the bottom line is that forbidding the use of drugs doesn't work, as shown by the failure of alcohol prohibition in the USA between the two wars. By making drugs illegal, we only sustain the criminality associated with their illegal trade.

If we legalised all drugs, most of the effort and money currently wasted on the losing war on drugs could be redirected towards more productive purposes, including educating people on how to deal with those substances[1].

The heavy taxes on alcohol, tobacco, and gambling mean, among other things, that smuggling of cigarettes into Australia remains a profitable trade. Therefore, I have no doubt that a legalised trade of opiates and cannabis would not completely remove their illegal trafficking. Still, it would significantly reduce an important source of income for terrorists and other criminal organisations.

Let's face it, we only make a distinction between, say, alcohol and cannabis because of cultural and traditional reasons. Such a dramatically different attitude towards different types of drugs is not based on Science and logic.

I think that governments should prevent people from harming others. That's why I welcome heavy fines given to people who drive in an altered state.

But I also think that governments should help those who harm themselves, and in my opinion, the best way to help addicts is to try to understand why they do it, and ensure that they have access to clean drugs and needles. If heroin were legal, deaths due to overdose would become a thing of the past, and

---

[1] I realise that I already made this point in a previous article.

most addicts would no longer need to resort to prostitution or crime to finance their dependency.

Addiction in itself should be treated as an illness, not a crime, and it should not be stigmatised. Some people can drink a lot without becoming alcoholics, while others can become addicted to alcohol very easily. Both genetic predisposition and societal factors play a role with any drug.

Many think: it will never happen to me. But they might be wrong. Sometimes, for some reason, people lose control over one of their needs or desires and begin over-drinking or over-eating, or become addicted to adrenaline or sex (or gambling). When will we step down from our pulpit and help them, rather than condemn them as sinners?

I just read an article in the latest issue of Time (April 2nd) that confirms how futile the war on drugs is. The title, "Incarceration Nation – The war on drugs has succeeded only in putting millions of Americans in jail", says it all.

Some figures are mind boggling: while Japan has 63 prisoners per 100,000 citizens, Germany 90, France 96, and Britain (one of the highest rates) 153, the USA has 760!

The population of US prisoners today is more than five times what it was in 1980. Still according to Times, this is due to the so-called war on drugs, as more than half of today's inmates were convicted on drug-related offences.

Another staggering figure: in 2009, 1.66 million Americans were arrested on drug charges, and 4/5 of them simply for possession.

Last year, a global commission on drug policy consisting of very authoritative politicians and former world-leaders stated[1]

---

[1] https://nation.time.com/2011/06/02/commission-drugs-win-war-on-drugs/

that "The global war on drugs has failed." Its main recommendation was to "encourage experimentation by governments with models of legal regulation of drugs to undermine the power of organized crime and safeguard the health and security of their citizens."

I couldn't agree more...

Originally posted in my blog in two parts on 2012-03-29 and 2012-03-30.

Aboriginality

I recently watched on TV a discussion about the concept of aboriginality. What is it and who should have the right to claim it?

When the whites came to Australia and claimed it for themselves, they almost completely destroyed Aboriginal culture and heritage. They did it in many ways, some of which were blatant and some more subtle. They did it by making a sport out of shooting Aborigines. They did it by taking away from their families those who had a white parent (thereby creating what is known as The Lost Generation). They did it by banning the use of Aboriginal languages and ceremonies. They did it by forcing Aborigines to abandon their traditional way of life. They did it by spreading diseases and alcohol. They did it by mocking and ridiculing black people.

Today, many descendants of the first Australians live in appalling conditions. On average, they live shorter lives than non-Aboriginal Australians. Their unemployment rate is shocking. And they end up and die in jail all too often.

It is not possible to erase what has already happened, but it is our collective obligation to provide to the Aborigines a better than fair chance to progress. I said "better than fair" because, after centuries of neglect and marginalisation, they need all the help they can get. Not as an act of charity, but as an act of justice and hope. They should receive help in finding ways of helping themselves.

We have in Australia a kind of affirmative action for Aborigines and Torres-Strait Islanders (Torres Strait is between Australia and Papua New Guinea). For example, all applications forms to apply for jobs with any level of

Australian government (local, state, or federal) include a box to tick if you can claim to descend from original Australians.

If you are recognised as an Aborigine, you have access to funding and grants that are unavailable to other Australians. This makes some Australians unhappy, but I fully support it. It is in my opinion a must.

That said, the fact that benefits are associated with being recognised as a person of Aboriginal descent clouds the issue of Aboriginality. Inevitably, some claim to be Aborigines to take advantage of the benefits, although they are not. Because of the benefits, the question of whether somebody is an Aborigine ceases to be purely a matter of identity, heritage, and culture.

Who decides whether you are an Aborigine? There are Aboriginal Councils and other organisations that can issue certificates of Aboriginality, but on which basis?

If somebody has the colour and the somatic traits of an Aborigine, speaks an Aboriginal language, and is known by the elders of the clan to which he belongs, there cannot be any doubts about his aboriginality.

Similarly, if one looks white and cannot prove to have any Aboriginal ancestry, there is a good chance that he is not an Aborigine.

But most cases are not so "black and white" (a pun!)

Some people only have an Aboriginal grandparent and look completely white, even with blue eyes and blond hair. And yet, having grown up in a family that was known in their neighbourhood to be Aboriginal, they consider themselves Aborigines.

Others were taken away from their Aboriginal mother and forcibly adopted by a white couple when they were babies.

They are dark-skinned, but have sometimes no idea where they were born, and might only know something of what it means being an Aborigine from what they have learned as adults.

As far as I know, in the USA, belonging to a tribe of Indian Americans is determined on the basis of a DNA test. Having a heritage and belonging to a culture has not much to do with DNA, does it? Is then a DNA test what is needed? If not, would it be fair to exclude people who know nothing about Aboriginal culture only because they were forcibly removed from their families?

I believe that we should define clear and measurable criteria and require that at least one of them is satisfied. Obviously, together with the desire of being recognised as an Aborigine because the last thing we want is to force people into drawers. The first possible criteria that come to mind are:

1. Traceability of ancestry to an Aboriginal person.
2. Presence of any Aboriginal DNA detected with a set probability, similarly to what is done in court to determine paternity.
3. Being recognised as a member by an Aboriginal clan by its elders.

Satisfying any one of them should suffice. I certainly left out something, but the point I want to make here is that the decision cannot be left to subjective opinion of people who have no association with the person who's applying to be recognised. The applicant shouldn't feel that his or her Aboriginality is arbitrarily questioned.

Like every law and regulation, also what I propose would be subject to abuse. For example, a single corrupt elder of a recognised Clan (there can be crooks anywhere) could be bribed into signing illegitimate certificates of Aboriginality. And any analysis, including a DNA test, can be faked.

But a clear set of rules would at least be verifiable. I'm convinced that the number of abuses would be reduced.

All of this says nothing about who should get support in preference to others because "greater need" is a fishy concept. But (just for the pleasure of throwing in a cliché) Rome wasn't built in a day...

Originally posted in my blog on 2012-08-15.

Kill, Kill, Kill!

In memory of Emilie Parker, one of many.

The second amendment to the US Constitution says:

A well regulated Militia, being necessary to the security of a free State, the right of the people to keep and bear Arms, shall not be infringed.

It was adopted on 15 December 1791.

Today, we wouldn't place a comma between subject and predicate, but grammar is not the only thing that has changed over the past 221 years.

In 1791, the USA had been independent for five years and counted fourteen states (Massachusetts, New Hampshire, Vermont, New York, Rhode Island, Connecticut, Pennsylvania, New Jersey, Delaware, Maryland, Virginia, North Carolina, South Carolina, and Georgia), plus the District of Columbia, two territories, and land disputed by Spain in the South and the U.K. in the North.

According to the 1791 census, the population of the fourteen states was 3,723,418, including 681,850 slaves. The current population of the 50 states is approximately 315 millions.

Much has been said about the American citizens' right to bear arms. I only want to make a couple of points.

Firstly, the US doesn't need a militia, as it was perhaps the case in 1791. They have federal, state, and local police, whose work is actually made more difficult and dangerous by all the weapons that are in circulation (an average of almost one per person).

Secondly, assault automatic weapons, contrary to what the lobby groups like the National Rifle Association claim, have nothing to do with sportsmanship. Cheap weapons designed for high fire power to kill at short range might be suitable for criminals, but have nothing to do with a civilised society.

I say: ban all automatic weapons, standardise and enforce registration laws, and make it difficult to buy ammunition.

Originally posted in my blog on 2012-12-17.

John Kerry's Negationism

Less than an hour ago, I saw the American Secretary of State John Kerry on TV. Talking about Bashar Al Assad, he stated something like "Since the use of poisonous gases was banned after WWI, only Hitler and Saddam Hussein used them".

He "forgot" to mention Italy and Japan. Everybody can condemn Nazi Germany and Saddam. But it wouldn't be proper to criticise two modern allies, would it?

Italy dropped mustard gas on Ethiopia in 1935, when Mussolini decided to give to Italy's king the additional title of Emperor of Ethiopia. According to Wikipedia, 150,000 people were killed, but even if you don't consider Wikipedia as a reliable source of information, it is clear that Italy killed many Ethipians with chemical warfare.

Still according to Wikipedia, Japan used chemical warfare in China in many occasions.

Allegedly for fear of retaliation, Germany made very limited use of gases during WWII. It doesn't seem entirely convincing because, by the time the allies had landed in Normandy, Nazi Germany had little to lose. In any case, Cyclon-B was used extensively in concentration camps to kill scores of people.

In conclusion, all three Axis powers used chemical warfare before or during WWII. Because of their racist ideologies or perhaps to avoid retaliation in kind, the gases were only used on blacks, Asians, and what the Germans classified as Untermenschen (subhumans: Jews, homosexuals, Romani people, and others).

I don't know about Japan, but I know that, even before the end of WWII, Italy was seen as a key piece of the frontier between Capitalism in the West and Communism in the East. It would have not been convenient for the Allies to institute an Italian version of the Nuremberg trials, especially considering that Italy's population included many Socialists and Communists

That's why all atrocities committed by Fascist Italy befor and during WWII were quietly ignored, including the gassing of thousands of Ethiopians (or the atrocities committed in Albania). The myth of the "good Italian soldier" was created and most Italians were happy to believe it.

John Kerry is only continuing the tradition of neatly dividing the world in goodies and badies according to what is convenient. He could have just stayed quiet, though...

Originally posted in my blog on 2013-09-08.

The World as I see it
Legalise them All

For years I have been of the opinion that we should legalise all drugs, light and heavy. I don't use any drug and only drink a little, perhaps a beer a month[1]. That wouldn't change if cannabis, narcotics, and what-have-you became available legally. I just don't understand why the state should prevent people from smoking or injecting what they want. They do it anyway. If drugs were legally available, the cost, both in terms of suffering and in terms of dollars, would be significantly reduced. And the thefts, spreding of diseases, and violence that surround the drug trade would disappear.

What the state should do is ensure that intoxicated people do not endanger other people's lives. And they are failing on that, because drunks cause many fatal car accidents and street fights. The issue is not whether somebody is drunk or high on dope. The issue is whether that person can sit behind a steering wheel or punch somebody. In this sense, alcohol is far more dangerous than, say, heroine. And yet, nobody is speaking of outlawing alcohol.

Can you imagine how much money would be freed if we stopped preventing people from buying drugs or growing marihuana plants in the backyard[2]? By legalising drugs, we would undermine most of the trafficking and the associated criminality and would save the lives of those who now die for overdose because they inject badly cut drugs[3]. And the government could tax drugs as they do now with alcoholic beverages.

---

1 It seems I couldn't stay away from this subject. But I don't like to merge the articles...

2 In the Australian Capital Territory it is now legal to grow a couple of plants for personal use.

3 At least free pill testing is finally beginning to be accepted.

Obviously, these considerations are not new, and I am sure that somebody will find counter-arguments for any argument I can bring, but we only need to look at history to know what we should do because humans have not significantly changed since the beginning of recorded history. In fact, we only need to go back less than one hundred years.

I am reading the book *The History of the Mafia* by Nigel Cawthorne, and have just arrived to where he writes about Prohibition and Al Capone. This is how that chapter begins:

When the Volstead Act banning the manufacture and sale of alcoholic beverages was passed in 1919, organized crime in America went mainstream. [...] it is estimated that 75 per cent of the population of the United States became client of bootleggers. It was big business. There had been 16,000 saloons in New York before the Volstead Act. These were replaced by 32,000 'speakeasies' (illegal drinking establishments). Britain's alcohol export to Canada rose six-fold and it was said that more intoxicating liquor was sent to Jamaica and Barbados than the population could possibly drink in a hundred years. During five years of Prohibition, 40 million gallons of wine and beer were seized. In 1925 alone, 173,000 illegal stills were impounded. This did nothing to stem the supply. And with the price of alcohol first doubling and then climbing to ten times what it had been before Prohibition, there was plenty of profit for the bootleggers.

Can you imagine how much effort and money it took to discover and seize millions of gallons of beverages and to close hundreds of thousands of illegal stills?

And it didn't really work. It only gave to organise crime a new market.

Perhaps not many know that Prohibition, besides in the USA, was tried in several countries (Russia, Finland, Iceland, Norway, to name the most significant). And it didn't work there either. It only helped organised crime.

You know what? I am optimistic. I believe that in a decade or two, at least in the western democracies, governments will realise that they have been mistaken in banning drugs[1]. Cannabis Sativa is a lovely leafy plant and I wouldn't mind growing it in my garden.

Originally posted in my blog on 2014-07-21.

---

1 Eleven years have passed since I wrote this article. There has been some progress...

The World as I see it

The World as I see it

Enough is Enough!

For how long are our governments going to put up with Israel's annihilation of Gaza?

The Israeli Army has hit UNrefugee camps, schools, and hospitals, but the governments of Australia, the USA, and who knows how many other countries don't make a pip.

For how long political alliances and lobbying-driven expediency are going to justify our leaders' acquiescence?

Gaza has been blockaded since 2007. This is inhumane and it should stop. But now the situation has deteriorated well beyond that. More than 1300 Palestinians have been killed, against 60 Israeli. Every death is a tragedy. Every death deprives a family of a loved one. But most of the 60 or so Israeli deaths are of soldiers who entered Gaza to bring destruction, while the majority of the Palestinian deads are civilians, including hundreds of children. Those with bloodied hands are Benjamin Netanyahu and his government[1].

How can anybody call such a massacre of innocent lives an assertion of Israel's right of self-defence? Hamas should stop firing rockets into Israel. There is no doubt about that. But even if Hamas's deadly game were a disingenuous attempt to stoke the conflict in order to score political and diplomatic sympathies, it couldn't possibly justify Israel's response.

Gaza is one of the most densely populated regions on Earth, and now Israel has declared a No-Go zone covering 30% of the whole territory. Additionally, Israel has destroyed the only power plant in Gaza, causing a permanent black-out in 80% of the strip. Without electricity, the fridges don't work, and most Palestinians are then forced to go out to buy food every day, further endangering their lives in the process.

---

1 A decade later and things have only become much worse.

The World as I see it

Self-preservation justifies a lot, but I am sure that many Israelis will be as horrified as I am at what is happening in Gaza.

During the second half of 1978, I was in Israel twice, for a total period of about two months. During my first trip there, I was for a month in Degania Aleph, the first Kibbutz established in Israel, were I met the young lady who was to become my wife. I have very fond memories of my staying in Israel and the last thing you could say about me is that I am an anti-Semite.

The resentment that is growing inside me is therefore not centred on the Jewish people, but on the criminal policies of the Israeli government. I am a pacifist and don't condone violence, especially when applied to the weak and the disadvantaged.

Obviously, I don't only condemn the actions of Netanyahu's government, but also Hamas strategy of confrontation and, most of all, the suicide bombings that have become an almost-daily occurrence in the Middle-East.

But although I don't excuse the recourse to terrorism, I do understand it. Perhaps more people should try to go beyong their one-way mindset and attempt to perceive the world from the point of view of suicide bombers. Those young Muslims feel like cornered animals, and lash out in desperation. The opulence of the Western world is for everyone to see on the TV screens, as is its moral decadence and its Hedonism, accompanied by hypocritical statements of values and virtues that have long be supplanted by greed and selfishness. Of course an increasing number of young Palestinian (and Syrian, Egyptian, Lebanese, Iraqi, ...) are attracted to those who speak of honour, purity, and a sacred mission to rid the world of the sinners. How can they resist that message, as misdirected and instrumentalised as it is?

We who live in rich western democracies should do our best to educate these youg people, give them hope, treat them with respect and compassion, not simply try to switch them off. And we should, first of all, start work at home by electing full human beings to govern us, rather than puppets of multinationals or robots only capable of uttering slogans.

I am sick and tired of listening to politicians who never answer a question, who only follow the party lines, who treat human beings as if they were inanimate objects, and who don't listen to anyone when they are in government only to then disagree with everything when they are in opposition. How I would love to be able to look at our elected representatives and feel proud of my country! But I am digressing...

Originally posted in my blog on 2014-07-31.

The World as I see it

RELIGION

The World as I see it

Religion and Child Molestation

I am sure that this will not be my last article on religion but, prompted by the worldwide scandals about catholic priests, I feel I have to talk about it.

I was born and grew up in Italy, where the catholic religion is embedded in the fabric of society. Even many parents who never go to church feel compelled to baptise their children. And the prime-time evening news show the pope or talk about him several times a week. In every classroom of every public school (at least, it used to be so when I grew up there), a crucifix hangs beside a picture of the current Italian president on the wall behind the teacher's desk.

Italian cities are full of catholic churches, and it is not uncommon to come across priests, friars, and nuns on the street. Not surprisingly, this is particularly true in Rome, where the pope lives, enclosed in his little totalitarian kingdom and protected by his Swiss guards. Incidentally, did you know that Rome is the only place where priests still wear a cassock instead of trousers? Although, to be completely fair, most of them wear trousers underneath, especially in winter.

As far as I can remember, I was never a believer. Probably it was so because my family was not religious either. I never saw my mother or my grandmother go to mass, and my father only went to church once a year, on palm Sunday, to buy a blessed branch of olive tree. But despite the lack of religious education I got at home, I was never allowed to say anything bad about God, Christ, Mary, or any saint. It was clearly a form of superstition: offending the saints would bring bad luck. The catholic faith, superstition, and pagan rites are not incompatible, as it is apparent in the worshipping of the virgin Mary and of patron saints throughout Italy. Also, if you enter a souvenir shop, you might find crosses and holy images beside pagan charms like those shown below.

In Italy, many things can be used as amulets. Horns (disguised penises), hunchbacks, the number 13, horseshoes, four-leaf clovers, and hare feet, to name the most common, are supposed to bring luck to their bearers.

Anyhow, I am digressing. It's just that superstition is so fascinating... I'll have to write separately about it.

Let's get back to talk about religion. As a consequence of Mussolini's 1929 agreement with the pope (the *Patti Lateranensi*), the syllabus of all Italian public schools includes one weekly hour of catholic religion. When I was a child, it was unthinkable for parents to request dispensation for their children. As a result, I calculated that during my thirteen years of schooling in Italy (at least at the time, the normal years of schooling in Italy were thirteen, not twelve like in Australia and in other countries), I attended some 400 hours of indoctrination into the catholic religion.

In primary school I had a little experience of [attempted] child molestation from the part of a friar. Our teacher of religion used to call a pupil to the front of the classroom to answer questions of catechism. Sometimes, he asked the boy (full segregation was the rule back then) to step up onto the platform on which his desk rested. The child then found himself facing the class while standing beside the teacher's chair. In those occasions, the teacher at times encircled the boy's body with his left arm or, behind the protection of his desk, pinched a buttock of the boy. I heard it from several classmates and it was well known within the class. That's why when once the teacher asked me to step up to his desk, I said that I preferred to remain where I was. The same teacher organised events for children in the nearby parish, but I never attended them. One can only speculate about what happened to the children who did.

I obviously condemn abuses against the weak and vulnerable. Therefore, I cannot excuse or tolerate the acts of the priests who take advantage of their community role to molest children. But condemning their actions doesn't prevent me from understanding them. The catholic church imposes wows of celibacy on its clergy. While most of us experience their first contacts with the other sex (or the same sex, or even an undefined one, no prejudice here), the young men who attend religious schools and seminaries are locked up within a repressive organisation that leave no space for their natural development. As long as the catholic church will insist on celibacy, a possible way for releasing the sexual drive of their priests will remain off-limits. The fact that protestant priests do not appear in the news like their catholic colleagues seems to confirm that celibacy is at the very least a contributing factor.

Anyhow, the pope should direct his bishops to pass any suspected case of child abuse to the police without any delay or preliminary internal investigation. And he should make this directive as public as possible.

Originally posted in my blog on 2010-07-14.

The World as I see it

The Ten Commandments

A lot could be said about the ten commandments, but my purpose here is to talk about the fact that the ten commandments in English, German, Italian, Spanish, and French are not exactly the same. The reason for choosing these languages is that they are the only languages I understand. The ten commandments appear three times in the Bible: in Exodus 20:2–17, Exodus 34:11–27, and Deuteronomy 5:6–21, and they are not identical. The official catholic version of the commandments is available online in the catechism pages published by the Vatican.[1]

The first commandment I would like to discuss is the 6th: "You Shall Not Commit Adultery". The literal English translation of the 6th commandment as it is expressed in Spanish (*No cometerás actos impuros*) is: "You shall not commit impure acts". Now, committing impure acts includes all sorts of activities that go well beyond adultery. Does that mean that Spanish catholics commit a sin when they masturbate at home but not when they are on vacation, say, in Britain? Or that Spanish people, regardless of where they are, commit a sin when masturbating but Britons can get away with it without having to confess it? It is interesting to note that, although the official Italian version of this commandment matches the English one, the version normally taught in Italy is identical to the Spanish version. And there are also French and German versions in circulation (*La pureté observeras en tes actes soigneusement* and *Du sollst nicht Unkeuschheit treiben*) that translate respectively into "You shall carefully practice purity" and "you shall not act

---

[1] https://www.vatican.va/archive/compendium_ccc/documents/archive_2005_compendium-ccc_en.html#The%20Ten%20Commandments

unchaste". All in all, it seems safest to adopt the English version!

Perhaps not surprisingly, considering the difficulties that the catholic church has with sex, also the 9th commandment ("You Shall Not Covet Your Neighbour's Wife") is not identical across the various languages. The Spanish are again the most restrictive. Their version (*No consentirás pensamientos ni deseos impuros*) translates into: "You shall not allow impure thoughts and desires". In Italian (*Non desiderare la donna d'altri*), the commandment is "You shall not covet the woman of others", which is more restrictive than the English version because it states that you commit a sin even if the woman you desire is engaged or involved with somebody else but without being married to him. I saw a French version of this commandment (*En pensées, désirs veilleras à rester pur entièrement*) that is very close to the Spanish one: "In thought, you shall be watchful and remain entirely pure in your desires". In any case, it seems that heterosexual women and homosexual men have it easy concerning the 9th commandment. At the very least, the church should consider making this commandment gender-neutral. But they are not good at this type of things, are they?

Some countries have it a bit more difficult with the 8th ("You Shall Not Bear False Witness Against Your Neighbour"): French and Italian commit a sin even when their false witnessing is not against their neighbour, but the Spanish (*No dirás falso testimonio ni mentirás*), as usual, have the strongest of all: "You shall not bear false witness or lie".

I don't think that in Spain there are more or worse sinners. Perhaps the commandments are strictest with the Spanish speakers because the catholic church thinks that they can get away with it...

I don't know whether the commandments as they are taught in France conform to the French official version, but I saw on the web a version (*Tes père et mère honoreras, tes supérieurs pareillement*) of the 4th ("Honour Your Father and Your Mother") that translated into: "You shall honour your father and your mother, as well as your superiors". I also saw a French version (*Meurtre et scandale éviteras, haine et colère pareillement*) of the 5th ("You Shall Not Kill") that translated into: "You shall avoid murder and scandals, as well as hate and anger". I let you judge the wisdom of such additional constraints. In any case, I lived in France for one and a half years, and you can trust me when I tell you that the French seem to get angry as easily as anybody else. Shame on their sinfulness!

I find it quite surprising that the commandments are different in different languages. After all, the Vatican is a fully centralised organisation, especially in matters of doctrine. It's not serious!

Originally posted in my blog on 2010-07-21.

The World as I see it

The World as I see it
A ban on Full Veils?

I believe that everybody, as long as they don't disadvantage or damage other people, should be able to say and do what they want. That's why I am in favour of reforms like those aimed at legalising drugs and at extending the validity of marriage contracts to homosexual couples. On the other hand, in what might be considered a sign of intolerance, I am in favour of preventing women from wearing in public full islamic veils.

At the time of writing, the Australian Prime Minister (Julia Gillard) and the leader of the opposition (Tony Abbott) agree that [some] Australians find the burqa (see left image) confronting. But neither leader is prepared to support a ban (and forfeit the votes of the growing muslim population). Obviously, although in Australia the debate is centred on the burqa, the same applies to the niqāb (see right image). For simplicity, in the rest of this article, I will use the term burqa to indicate both the actual burqa and the niqāb.

The World as I see it

A couple of days ago, a judge in Western Australia asked a woman wearing a burqa and intending to give testimony in a court case to reveal her face. This made her feel very uncomfortable, but in such cases Islam allows even the most conservative women to remove their veil. Therefore, strictly speaking, the argument that the burqa must be banned for legal and security purposes is not a valid one. People have to remove their integral motorcycle helmets when entering a bank, and the same rule applies to fully veiled women. Still, despite the fact that the law requires it and Islam does not forbid it, I expect that few bank employees, if any, will be prepared to ask a veiled woman to show her face. A general ban would solve the issue.

A terrorist could use a burqa to hide an explosive vest and then detonate the bomb in a crowded place. Australia is not [yet] a target of terrorist attacks, but the question is justified in principle. But if we ban the burqa in all crowded public places, fully veiled women could only walk in desolated back alleys. We might as well ban the burqa in every public place and be done with it. At the very least, it would make law enforcement easier.

That said, let's face it, the banning of the burqa is more than just a security issue. From a security point of view, it might even be argued that, by banning the burqa in Australia, we might encourage the very same acts of terrorism that the ban of the burqa is meant to protect us from.

In fact, I would like to see the burqa banned in Australia because it is a tool of repression, used for centuries to subjugate women. The imposition of the burqa goes together with keeping the women away from schools, stoning them to death when they are accused of being unfaithful to their husbands, mutilating them to remove any hope of sexual pleasure, and effectively consider them like cattle. The women who wear a burqa in Australia can go to school, are not mutilated, and neither are they stoned to death. Therefore, it could be argued that we don't have the right to force them to abandon their traditional dress. Aren't we being arrogant in thinking that we know what's better for them? What if they don't want to be "liberated"? Further, if we want to progress as a tolerant and open society, shouldn't we accept the burqa as the manifestation of religious beliefs? Is there really a difference between wearing a golden cross around the neck (something that, FYI, is forbidden in Saudi Arabia) and covering the face? I believe there is.

During an email discussion about the burqa, somebody once asked me whether I was in favour of banning prostitution and pornography as well. He argued that they demeaned women perhaps more than the burqa, implicitly suggesting that I was just being conservative and intolerant. In general, I believe that prostitution and pornography are demeaning for the people who provide it, whether they are women or not. And as in the case of the Burqa, some (or many) of them have no interest in being "saved". But the sex industry and the burqa are two different types of issues because the existence of prostitution is rooted in our biology. There have been men prepared to pay for sex in all cultures and probably even before money was invented. What we must do is to ensure that nobody is forced into prostitution and that people who work in the sex industry are protected from racketeering and violence. I know. It is difficult to decide who is forced and who is not. But concerning the burqa, how many of the women who wear it in Australia would do so if they had not been conditioned from birth or forced by their male companions and relatives?

As far as I know (please correct me if I am wrong) women of all other cultures use the most diverse techniques to make themselves attractive to the healthiest, strongest, and most successful men. This is not demeaning. It is natural. Exactly as men find most attractive the women who are shaped to be good child-bearers. The complete hiding of the female body is therefore unnatural. It is the result of a culture in which women change hands from fathers and brothers to husbands as if they were objects. It is not surprising that the Taliban want to keep them ignorant to the point of illiteracy.

Many laws exist to protect the weaker elements in our society from abuse. I see the banning of the burqa as one of those laws. I know the argument of the "slippery slope": if we start syndicating what people are allowed to wear, what do we ban next? We must be vigilant, but I still believe that the burqa has no place in a modern liberal society.

For the record, there are already laws that limit the way we dress in public. For example, try to walk into a shopping centre wearing a hat, socks, shoes, and nothing else. You can rest assured that you will be arrested and fined. Some people would feel uncomfortable sitting in a bus beside a naked person, but why is it enough to justify the banning of nudity? I don't find banning the burqa more restrictive than banning nudity.

In a truly free society, women (and, obviously, men) should be allowed to wear what they want. But today there are still men who impose unnatural rules on their daughters, sisters, and wives. I consider it a duty of our legislators to stop such practices. Hopefully, one day, these pockets of medieval mentality will disappear, and women and men will finally be able to work side by side as equals (dressed or undressed as they like).

Originally posted in my blog on 2010-08-06.

The Responsibility of the Pope

I just finished watching the Australian talk show Q&A (Questions and Answers), in which a panel of five well known people (politicians, intellectuals, journalists, etc.) answers questions asked by the public. One of the panelists, Geoffrey Robertson QC, is known to have suggested that the Pope should be formally held responsible for the abuses of catholic priests against children. During the programme, he was asked to explain why the pope should be held accountable for what he clearly condemns. Obviously, being a lawyer, he answered in a very articulate manner, but one sentence impressed me as being central to his argument, and I feel compelled to report it here. He said: "If you have got the power to stop a crime, you have the duty to do it."

This is a very compelling statement and, in my opinion, at the heart of the issue. For years the catholic church has been transferring to other dioceses priests who had been accused of abusing children. The fact that the pope recently apologised for the abuses doesn't cut it. If he really wanted to stop them, he could, right now. He would only need to tell the bishops that any case of suspected abuse should be transferred to the local police. Easy. As long as he will fail to do so, he will make himself an accomplice of the crime after the fact.

Originally posted in my blog on 2010-10-04.

Is This True about Islam?

After viewing a YouTube video that makes statements about Islam (since removed), I decided to write about its three key points. Before publishing this article, I asked myself whether it would be offensive to Muslims in any way, but I don't see how.

1. People who haven't read the Qur'an (i.e., the majority of us, me included, although I did buy it and read some of it) assume that it is a book comparable to the Bible, but it is not so. The Bible was authored by several people over a period of centuries, and contains culture, history, parables, and allegories. The Qur'an, on the other hand, was written by a single person and focuses on imperatives. Moreover, in the Qur'an it is stated that, if there are contradictions, the later verse supersedes any previous differing one. You can only take or refuse the Qur'an in its entirety. As it happens, the mild and peaceful verses cited by moderate Muslims tend to appear at the beginning and are superseded by more violent verses. Therefore, the Qur'an is described to us as a much more peaceful book than it actually is.

2. Islam is not simply a religion. Islamic doctrine and practice encompass all aspects of society including: belief and ritual worship, economic transactions, contracts, morals and manners, and crime and punishment. Shari'ah permits wife beating, honour killing, and, literally, an eye for and eye punishment. It mandates death for homosexuals, apostates, adulterers, and critics of Allah, Muhammad, the Qur'an, and Islam. Global imposition of Islamic doctrine and practice is a religious duty, not a matter of choice.

3. Muslims are explicitly allowed to deceive non-Muslims to protect and advance the imposition of Islam. The

author of the video stated that Muslim leaders have been known to deliver different messages when talking in English than they delivered when talking in Arabic.

I don't know [yet] whether these statements are correct or not. If they are, it could mean that what we call Islamic fundamentalists could in fact be closer to the correct doctrine of Islam than the so-called moderates. Or it could mean that the moderates are not so moderate after all and only express themselves in peaceful terms because it is the best way to pursue their goal of world islamisation.

Honestly, I don't know what to think. I should read more of the Qur'an, but can I trust its translations?

Originally posted in my blog on 2010-10-12.

The World as I see it

The Catholic Church and Its Miracles

Reading "The Case of the Pope" by Geoffrey Robertson QC I am discovering a lot of interesting facts concerning the current pope and the way in which the Vatican operates. It was written in a somewhat boring way and contains several repetitions, but I recommend it to both catholics and non-catholics.

The "Vatican City" is the tiny enclave in Rome where the pope lives, and "The Holy See" is the worldwide governing body of the Roman Catholic Church. They claim that together they represent a sovereign state as a matter of international law.

For simplicity, I will use here the term "Vatican" to indicate either or both of them.

The Vatican participates to the work of the UN as a non-member state. Being recognised as a state gives to the Vatican several advantages compared to other religions. Most importantly, it provides sovereign immunity to itself and to its head of state from any legal action. Additionally, it gives access to United Nations' agencies, conferences, and conventions to promote its 'apostolic mission'.

Now, whether an entity constitutes a sovereign state or not is defined in the text ratified at the Montevideo Convention on the Rights and Duties of States of 1933[1]. It was the Seventh International Conference of American States and, although Bolivia didn't sign it and some other states ratified it with reservations, it merely restated and codified customary international law. As such, it is applicable worldwide. For example, the European Union's Arbitration Commission of

---

1 Full text of the convention:
  http://www.taiwandocuments.org/montevideo01.htm

the Peace Conference on the former Yugoslavia, followed it in the early 1990s.

In a nutshell, the Montevideo Convention reaffirmed that an entity is a state if it has:

- a permanent population,
- a defined territory,
- a government,
- the capacity to enter into relations with the other states.

The Vatican has a government and the capacity to enter relations with other states, but it could be argued that it doesn't have a territory. The land occupied by the Vatican (less than half a square kilometre) was granted by Mussolini to the pope in 1929. The Catholic religion was made the Italian 'religion of state', and the Vatican remained subjected to Italian law, albeit with some concessions and privileges. The *Concordato* signed by Mussolini and the Vatican was the first of a series of agreements between a state and the Catholic Church, namely, a non-state entity. How can the Vatican claim to be a state on the basis of such agreements?

In any case, the Vatican certainly doesn't have a permanent population, unless one accepts the idea that a single male vowed to celibacy constitutes a population.

Thanks to its alleged statehood, the Vatican has been able to influence the policies of many states in a way that is not available to other religions. According to the traditional Catholic religion, homosexuals are evil, gay marriages are evil and insidious, abortion is a deadly sin that should be placed beyond the reach of women, women are damned for eternity if they use any form of contraception, IVF embryo experimentation is evil, condoms should be banned in HIV/AIDS-ravaged countries, sex should only be enjoyed by married heterosexual couples as a means for having children, viewing of pornography or donation of sperm are to be condemned, as well as pre-natal scans, mother surrogacy, and euthanasia.

Here in Australia, following the recent canonisation of Mary MacKillop, many politicians expressed on the media how pleased they were that Australia finally had their catholic saint. This included our declared atheist Prime Minister. I personally found the whole theatre as a glorification of superstition.

The last thing I want is to risk to have my blog censored but, although a catholic might find my sentence offensive, I believe that such a feeling would be unjustified. My sentence that believing in miracles is in my opinion superstition is a perfectly valid statement from a scientific point of view. The Free Dictionary by Farlex[1] gives the following definition of superstition: "An irrational belief that an object, action, or circumstance not logically related to a course of events influences its outcome."

A link between a 'holy intervention' (for lack of a better term) and the inexplicable healing of a deadly disease is only postulated 'by exclusion': a miracle is recognised if the claimant states that [s]he directed her/his prayers towards a particular person and no scientific explanation of the healing can be found.

In other words, the Catholic Church does not prove that the particular saint effected the cure in response to prayers, but only that the contrary cannot be demonstrated. In any Natural Science, including Medicine, you cannot claim something to be true simply because you are unable to prove that it is false.

---

1 https://www.thefreedictionary.com/superstition

In conclusion, prayers and the healing of a person are not logically related, and to believe otherwise is superstitious.

I am sure that there are many cases of unexplained healing that baffle the doctors. Are they undeclared miracles? Or rather, more reasonably, events that go beyond our current understanding of the human body?

I heard from an authoritative font of a paratrooper who was unharmed after a fall in which his parachute didn't open (and its reserve neither). What if he had said that while he was falling he had prayed his favourite saint to save him? Would have that event qualified as a miracle? As far as I know, he didn't make the claim, but where do you draw the line?

Originally posted in my blog on 2010-10-21.

It's a Matter of Faith

Yesterday, a friend of mine who defines himself as a creation-believing-Christian suggested that I attend a lecture titled *Creation: The Missing Link*. I couldn't resist replying with a tirade against Creationism. Here it is.

The results in Molecular Biology have demonstrated beyond any reasonable doubt that evolution is sufficient to explain the variety of species that exist (or have gone extinct). Last December, I read a very detailed and documented book that demonstrates just that: *The Making of the Fittest - DNA and the ultimate forensic record of evolution*, by Sean B. Carroll.

Faith and Science are two different things. Creationism and Intelligent Design can explain everything. I know. But the best proofs they can count on are tautological.

Peer-reviewed published Science is not infallible, but when the body of evidence grows over decades and no measure, experiment, or discovery invalidates a theory, the probability that the theory is false is immensely reduced. Relativity, for example, is a theory and, as such, it could be refined in future, exactly as Relativity itself refined Newtonian Mechanics. But, after so many confirmations, it cannot ever be invalidated, exactly as Newtons theories have not been.

The Global Positioning System only works because the clocks on the satellites are adjusted to take into account Relativity. The Cosmological Constant introduced and then repudiated by Einstein to avoid divergence of his formulae has been re-introduced to be able to avoid contradiction with the fact that the universe is expanding at an accelerating rate. Dark Energy and the Cosmological Constant are ad-hoc solutions to explain (without actually explaining anything) the expansion of the universe. This is a clear indication the Relativity as we know it is part of a more general theory that will explain the universe without fudging the formulae. But that doesn't invalidate Relativity at all.

All theories go through successive refinements and generalisations.

Another "fudge" in Science that I know of is the "renormalisation" used in Quantum Field Theory to get rid of infinities (a bit like saying that $0/0 = 1$!). Again, it means that the theory will probably be refined in future (unless it becomes a particular case of a more general theory that doesn't need renormalisation). Meanwhile, Quantum Theory has explained to us semiconductors, superconductivity, superfluidity, and a host of other useful stuff.

Evolution is yet another theory and, like Newtonian Mechanics, Relativity, and Quantum Mechanics, will probably be refined in future. But meanwhile, it explains the diversity of Nature without need for any external intervention. And the aim of any explanation must be to be parsimonious: don't do anything more than necessary to achieve a certain result. The fewer the ad-hoc factors invoked to explain something, the better (Occam's Razor).

This does not (and I don't see why it should) prevent you from believing that the laws of Physics are what they are because a God invented them and then set the universal constants exactly to the value they currently have. But, as I said, it is then a matter of Faith, not of Science.

Sometimes (but very very very seldom! ;-) I wish I believed in God. I know it can be of great comfort. But I don't believe in God, and don't think I ever will (although, obviously, the future cannot be really predicted...)

In the book "Religion for Atheists", the philosopher Alain De Botton (of whom you can see an interview with him on the ABC 7.30 Report's website), despite being a staunched

Atheist, claims that we should respect religion and try to learn from it, rather than dismiss it. He says that Religion does certain thing very well and that we miss some of them in our modern secular world. I just watched the interview on the web and it is absolutely worth watching. I strongly encourage you to do so. Alain is not just brilliant and articulate. He is also caring. I can tell you this: if everybody thought like him, religious or atheist, I doubt that there would be any religious persecution in this world.

Originally posted in my blog on 2012-02-28.

The World as I see it

Faith and Buddhism

I've started meeting with a Buddhist group. I'm an atheist, and that's not going to change. But I don't see Buddhism as a religion, regardless of what Wikipedia says.

I am an atheist because I don't believe that some God has created the universe and/or has an interest in human affairs. I realise that my non-believing in God is as unjustified as the belief of Catholics, Muslims, and Jews that a God exists. Without any way of scientifically proving or disproving the existence of God (or Gods), the only logical position to hold is Agnosticism.

That notwithstanding, I don't believe that a God exists. This makes me as illogical as any believer. It annoys me a bit at an intellectual level, but I can't help it. I also believe that it makes sense to speak of being good and virtuous (there you have a word that is completely out of fashion!), and that being good is ultimately associated to being happy or, at the very least, that you cannot be completely happy if you behave badly.

But what is good and what is bad? Or, to see it from the point of view of change, which pervades all our existences, what is better and what is worse? And more dramatically, what is right and what is wrong? I don't know. I have been asking myself those same questions all my adult life. Does it make sense at all to speak about right and wrong? It sounds so dogmatic...

And yet, as I said, I do believe that it makes sense to distinguish between good actions and bad actions. After all, there is an almost universal agreement that lying, stealing, and killing are not thing that one should do.

Logical thinking doesn't help much in these moral matters. That's why when somebody asks me why I am a vegetarian, I reply that it feels right to me. And I'm very strict as well (uncompromising, if you like), which is a very illogical position to hold. I became vegetarian when I started looking for ways of becoming a better person. Did it work? I wouldn't know, but I still think that it is right for me.

I suppose, following such a self-chosen rule helps me keep chaos at bay, whatever that means.

I base all my relationships on respect, and trust comes natural to me, which obviously exposes me to abuse. Like when a friend of a friend asked me to lend him a non-negligible amount of money (more than a month of my pay). I hesitated, because I didn't really know that person and, actually, I didn't like him. I thought I might never see my money again. But then, I asked myself: do I want to be the type of person who says no? I'd be just one more selfish bastard. But if I trust this person, I will be better for it, regardless of whether I will one day get my money back or not. Well, you guessed it: I only got back a fraction of what I lent, and that person even accused me of helping him only because I was paternalistic.

I still remember it three and a half decades later, and it still annoys me, but I know I did the right thing.

My father, whom I, regrettably, didn't appreciate enough when he was alive, also was a trusting man. I remember that he once acted as the guarantor for a loan to a relative, and then found himself in an extremely tight spot when that relative defaulted on the repayments. My father was a good man. I am very sorry I never told him.

But I'm digressing, as usual.

All three major religions I mentioned above have prophets as emissaries of their Gods. Buddha was not a prophet, though, because Buddhism has no God. According to some tradition, some two and a half millennia ago, a man developed over the course of decades a way of reaching complete happiness. On request of others, he taught his method, thereby starting the Buddhist tradition.

I have read a bit about Buddhism, but I don't really know much about it. What I know is that when I went to Canberra's centre of Diamond Way Buddhism, I found myself surrounded by great people. Marvellous human beings. Never in my life had I ever met a group of people so open, so ready to welcome me among them, so eager to help without imposing anything in exchange.

Something clicked at once between us.

Theravada Buddhism teaches you techniques; in Mahayana Buddhism, the teachers act as examples; and in the Vajrayana tradition of Buddhism, to which the Diamond Way belongs, there is more emphasis on the teachers, who are supposed to inspire you.

As one of my newly-found friends said: trust must be earned. You are not expected to believe a teacher upfront. But when you see that his teachings help you again and again, you are bound to listen very carefully to what he says, and expect that a further teaching will also help you. This is what trust means.

Well, I'm new to this, but I do believe that I have in me the capability of being completely happy, and I'm willing to give it a try.

Originally posted in my blog on 2013-02-14.

The World as I see it

ARTIFICIAL INTELLIGENCE AND POSTHUMANISM

The World as I see it

The Future of Being Human

We are entering a new phase of human evolution. The next few decades will mark the end of humanity as we know it today.

The genus Homo has been around for a couple of million years. Some 130,000 years ago the species Homo Sapiens developed in Africa and begun spreading to the rest of the world. They were the direct ancestors of all human beings living on earth today (although the interbreeding with other Human species like the Neanderthals added some percent of non-Sapiens DNA). The differences that we see today between the various ethnic groups are the result of living under very different environmental conditions in the ensuing millennia. They account for some 40 genes out of a total of 40,000. The resulting rate of genetic change is one gene every 20 to 30 thousand years.

For example, only few adults had the gene necessary for digesting milk derivatives when humans learnt how to domesticate and breed animals. The advantage of being able to utilise such a rich source of proteins and nutrients set in motion a darwinian selection in favour of that gene. But the natural evolution is so slow that today, 10,000 years later, more than half of the world population is still unable to digest lactose.

While our anatomy and genetic makeup require millennia to show any change, the same does not apply to our way of life. Spurned by a flood of scientific and technological innovations, our society and culture have changed at an increasing speed over our recorded history. The construction of the great pyramids in Egypt occurred 200 generations ago. The Roman Empire lasted 60 generations and fell a little more than 50 generations ago. Somewhat less than 23 generations ago Gutenberg built his first printing press. Thomas Savery patented the first steam engine some 12 generations ago.

The list is endless, but up to the last four generations, at the end of the 19th century, changes occurred at a pace we could keep up with. Till then, the conflicts between generations, which have probably always existed, were part of the natural growing process of the individual. This is no longer true. Electric street lighting, radio, motorcars, and airplanes appeared in the decade spanning across the 19th and 20th centuries. The whole 20th century was a roller-coaster ride towards the future. Society changed so quickly that the generational gap became a real fracture.

Today, change has become an integral part of our society, and the rate of change itself keeps increasing. We are accelerating towards our future, not just getting there at constant speed and at a sedate pace.

It makes sense. As any new technology generates a palette of new possibilities, its introduction results in a cascading effect comparable to that of compound interest. Innovation feeds on itself in an explosive way, further accelerated by the increasing efficiency and decreasing cost of information distribution.

Many people in the developed countries have access to technological marvels their parents wouldn't have even dreamed of. But all those new technologies are modifying our society at a deep level. Ultimately, they will change the way in which we see ourselves. One thing is clear: computers have entered our everyday life to stay.

These changes are still subtle. Some of us still believe they could switch all the gadgets off and retire to a life close to nature. But this is an illusion. In reality, computers already dictate most aspects of our existence. For most people they have become modern tyrants, or oracles, which provide unquestionable and undisputable answers. So many times we hear that something is not possible because a computer program doesn't allow it. Soon a computer generated image with synthesised voice and automatic speech recognition will replace the last human operators. It is technically possible today and it will become an everyday's fact of life as the cost of computing keeps decreasing. No more arguing with operators then...

Eventually, unless we do something about it, the machines will become the real masters of our lives. To avoid succumbing to them, we will have to learn how to transcend our current biological limits. We will need to evolve into a new species, the Homo Novus. This will be possible thanks to the technologies that some of our leading scientists are developing right now.

The first of these new technologies is the merging of our bodies with artificial parts and in particulars with computers. It will affect our very nature as human beings. We understand always better how information is transmitted and stored in our brains. We are already able to build simple interfaces to control computers with our thoughts. We can also implant chips capable of preventing epileptic crises or reducing the most debilitating effects of Parkinson's disease. It is only a matter of time before these technologies will become available to the general public and for all sorts of applications.

The second new technology is genetic engineering applied to the human genome. Many governments are grappling with the problem of preventing scientists from cloning and altering human genes or splicing genes from other species into human embryonic cells. They will lose that battle because it is not possible to control what happens in all laboratories. It is not even possible to know where all the laboratories are. Moreover, as it happened with fiscal paradises and off-shore abortion clinics, many countries will open their doors to genetic research banned elsewhere. And being a scientist means having the insatiable desire to explore the boundaries of what is possible.

And then, there is nanotechnology. That is, the extreme miniaturisation of mechanical devices to the point that they can even operate at the molecular level.

The combined effects of these technologies will change humanity. Perhaps it will not be a utopian society without differences or hunger, but it will still be a world full of new opportunities and wonders.

Originally posted in my blog on 2010-07-21.

Machines that Can Think

Only a few decades ago computers filled up entire rooms and only accepted inputs via switches on their front panels or punched cards. The continuing increase in processing power and decrease in size has made possible to fit computers into smaller and smaller packages. In two decades we have gone from the size of a small suitcase to something comparable in size with a pack of cigarettes.

Computers are devices consisting of many electronic switches packed into integrated circuits. As the simplest electronic switch is the transistor, it makes sense to measure computing power in terms of transistors per integrated circuit. The more transistors we manage to pack into chips, the more powerful and small our computers become.

In 1965 Gordon Moore, a co-founder of Intel, estimated that chip density was doubling every year. Figure 1[1], based on more than three decades of data, shows that the doubling actually occurs every 24 months or so. Although lower than the original estimate, such a rate of increase still means an explosion of computing power.

But computing power is a very generic term. The speed at which computers can perform calculations is not just related to the number of transistors you manage to squeeze into their microprocessors, but also to how quickly you operate them. That's why the MHz (Megahertz = 1 million cycles per second) and GHz (Gigaherz = 1 billion cycles/s) of clocking frequencies advertised by the computer manufacturers are important in determining how fast your programs will execute.

---

1 Freely licensed by Wikimedia Commons as http://commons.wikimedia.org/wiki/File:Moore_Law_diagram_%282004%29.png

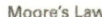

The World as I see it

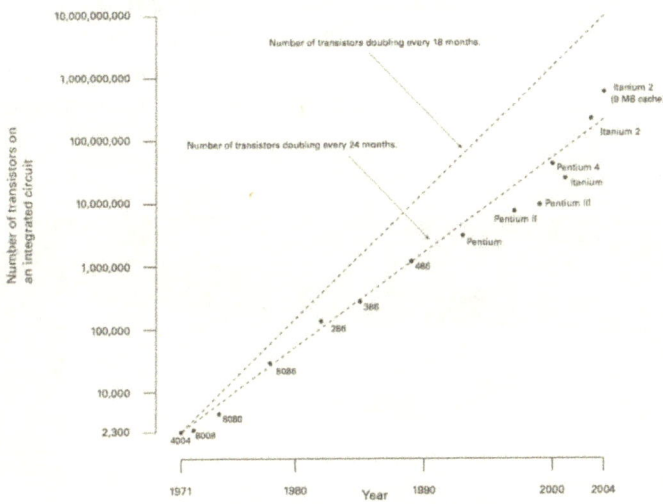

Figure 1: Moore's Law

Today's programs require a lot of memory to run. If the computers don't have enough of it, they are forced to juggle data in such a way that their performance significantly drops. As memory chips, like all integrated circuits, follow Moore's law, larger amounts of memory packaged more tightly and running faster have become available. This has further increased the efficiency of computers.

To top it off, it turns out that Moore's two-year doubling also applies to computer clocking. That's why the power of modern computers increases at the neck-breaking rate we observe today.

Ray Kurzweil, in his book *The Singularity is Near*, looks at the evolution through time of the number of calculations per second you can buy for 1,000 US dollars. This indicator of computing power is more useful than a straight count of transistors in a chip. It measures what computers can do at a certain cost, rather than how complex they are. Kurzweil's study includes forty-nine systems spanning in time the whole twentieth century. The results (see Figure 2[1]) show continuity across all technologies used to construct computational machines.

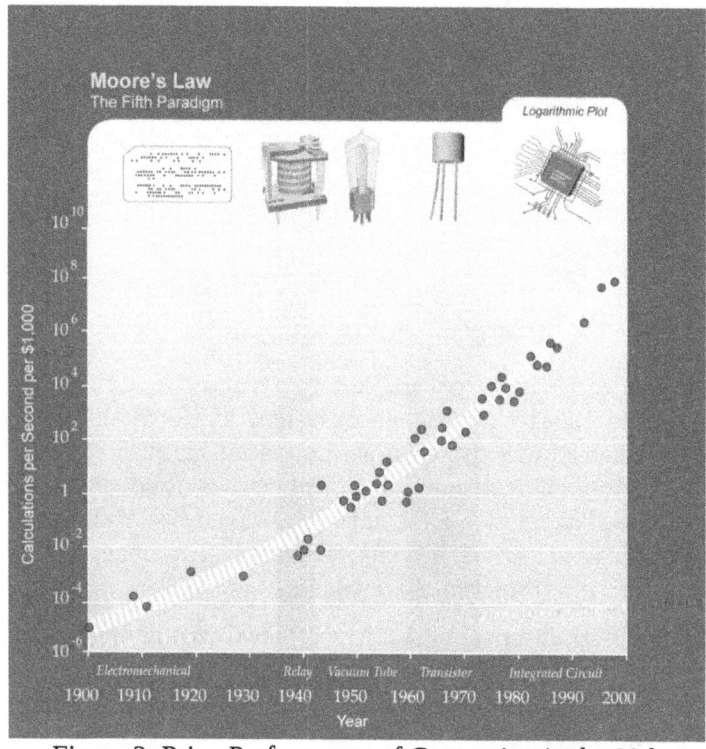

Figure 2: Price-Performance of Computing in the 20th Century

---

[1] Freely licensed by Wikimedia Commons as http://en.wikipedia.org/wiki/Image:PPTMooresLawai.jpg

At least three independent factors contribute to the trend displayed in Kurzweil's plot. Firstly, the number of calculations per second increases as new architectures take advantage of the increasing number of transistors available in individual computer chips. Secondly, calculations quicken as clock speeds of computers increase according to their own Moore's law. Thirdly, more efficient manufacturing processes and larger production batches reduce prices.

Notice that the plot shown in Figure 2 curves up. This means that the time necessary to double the number of computations per second per $1,000 has itself shrunk over the decades. It was two years at the beginning of the century but decreased to a single year towards its end. That is, the same amount of money will buy you in one year a computer twice as powerful as the computer you could buy now.

In 2007 Intel introduced a family of microprocessors with a transistor size of 45 nm (1 nanometer = one billionth of a metre, or one millionth of a millimeter), corresponding to a few hundred atoms (atoms have diameters of one to three tenths of a nm). In the same year Intel also announced a further reduction of transistor size to 32 nm planned for production in 2009. The photolithographic techniques used to produce computer chips by engraving increasingly small patterns on silicon wafers are probably close to reaching their physical limits. Therefore, it is not clear for how long the chip manufacturers will be able to shrink the transistor size.

But there are techniques to pack more transistors into a single processor. In 2007 IBM announced a chip-stacking technology that makes possible to build three-dimensional chips, as opposed to the current flat layouts. This will increase the number of transistors packed into a processor and reduce the distance between parts of the chip, thereby increasing internal communication speed.

Another way of increasing processing power is to do calculations in parallel. The most powerful PCs on the market at the time of writing have quad-core microprocessors. This means that a single microprocessor contains in fact four processing units sharing the load. But molecular and quantum computers will be able to execute trillions of operations simultaneously. That will sustain the exponential growth of computing power for decades to come.

A molecular computer stores and processes data using DNA fragments or other organic molecules. DNA (deoxyribonucleic acid) is the molecule that encodes the genetic instructions of living organisms, including ourselves. It consists of two chains of basic components (Adenine, Thymine, Guanine, and Cytosine) linked in pairs. A molecular computer exploits the fact that a sequence of base pairs can encode any information, exactly like a sequence of zeroes and ones in a digital computer.

To solve a problem with a DNA computer, you encode your input data in DNA fragments and let them join with each other. You then apply one or more enzymes which represent the constraints of the problem you are trying to solve. These enzymes destroy some sequences and leave other sequences unchanged. If you choose the correct enzymes, the sequences left at the end of the process represent the solution — or solutions — of the problem. This might sound tricky, but the potential is enormous because all possible solutions form simultaneously. This is the essence of parallelism. Also consider that the base pairs have a size of 0.33 nm, one hundred and fifty times smaller than the transistors packed in today's most advanced microprocessors. This means that DNA computers are much more densely packed than computers based on silicon.

This technique is still in its infancy, but it is reasonable to expect that in a few years the complexity of the process will be hidden inside bio-chips. Already in October 2006, researchers from Columbia University Medical Center and the University of New Mexico built a DNA-based integrated circuit with one hundred logic elements.

Quantum computers will achieve a level of parallelism even higher than that of molecular computing. While digital computers operate with bits, which can only assume the values 0 and 1, quantum computers operate with quantum bits — called for brevity qubits — which can have simultaneously the values 0 and 1.

To explain it rigorously, I would have to introduce quantum mechanics, but that would be outside the scope of this article. I will instead give you an idea of how that is possible by using a simple example.

Consider a spinning top. You could associate 0 to a clockwise spin and 1 to a counterclockwise spin. If you look at the top, you are able to see whether the spin is 0 or 1. The fact that you look at the top doesn't change its spinning status. You see 0 if the spin is 0 and 1 if the spin is 1. You could use a bit in the memory of a digital computer to record the spin status of the top.

The situation is completely different at the atomic and subatomic level, where quantum mechanics applies. Electrons have a property called spin, which can only have the values $½$ and $-½$. If you don't observe the electron, its spin is undefined. This is different from the case of the top, where the spin was defined regardless of whether you looked at it or not. By observing the spin of an electron, you force it to be either $½$ or $-½$. In other words, the act of observing the electron sets its spin to a defined value. You can use the spin status of an electron as a qubit of a quantum computer, with 0 corresponding to a spin of $½$ and 1 to a spin of $-½$.

The big advantage of quantum computing is that you can simultaneously represent several data values with a single set of qubits. This is possible because each qubit can hold an undefined value. But the same property of qubits also causes problems. First of all, it is difficult to handle qubits because they only hold their undefined state if you don't observe them. Secondly, the results obtained from a quantum computer are probabilistic. In other words, if you repeat the same calculation you can get different results, each with its frequency of occurrence.

The researchers are making progress in setting up qubits and finding ways of using them. For example, the company D-Wave introduced in February 2007 a 16-qubit quantum computer based on superconductors. Towards the end of the same year, they then demonstrated a 28-qubit quantum computer and announced their plan to reach 1024 qubits by the end of 2008.

It will take several years before molecular and quantum computers will become commonplace, but it will happen. Computers will certainly overtake the processing capacity of the human brain during our lifetime.

Hans Moravec, research professor at the Robotic Institute of Carnegie Mellon University, estimates that computer hardware will match the human brain in 2020. Kurzweil, in the already cited book, calculates that a computer performing ten million billion calculations per second — a one followed by sixteen zeroes, or 10^{16} — would be capable of simulating a human brain.

Well, on May 25th, 2008, IBM's Roadrunner supercomputer became the first computer in the world performing more than one million billion calculations per second. It took four years to build and two more years to make it fully operational. The National Nuclear Security Administration of the U.S.

The World as I see it

Department of Energy operates the Roadrunner at the Los Alamos National Laboratory, in New Mexico. They use it to simulate complex technical, scientific, and financial events and phenomena, like the aging of nuclear materials.

It will only take another handful of years before a supercomputer ten times as powerful as Roadrunner will come into existence. It will happen. And within the next decades some American institution will use it to emulate the functions of a human brain. Can we say that such a machine will think? My answer is a definite yes.

Alan Turing, in his article Computing Machinery and Intelligence of 1950[1], proposed a way for deciding whether a machine is capable of thinking. His proposal is known today as the Turing test and goes as follows. We ask as many questions as we like both to the machine being tested and to a person. As a result, we receive two sets of written answers, one from the machine and one from the person. If we cannot decide which set was provided by the machine, we should conclude that the machine is a thinking artificial being. The test is successfully passed if a computer is mistaken for a human more than 30% of the time during a series of five-minute keyboard conversations.

We should only pose questions that a human being could reasonably answer. If we asked to perform very complex mathematical calculation, the person would not be able to provide correct answers in a reasonable amount of time. It would then be easy to identify the machine. Unless, that is, the machine were aware of our limitations and provided wrong answers in order to appear human.

From now on, I will use the term AI (Artificial Intelligence) to indicate a machine capable of passing the Turing test. It seems only fair. I predict that the first AI will become operational

---

[1] In the journal Mind, Vol. 59, No. 236, October 1950.

around 2015[1], at a price of a few million dollars. Then, in another decade or so, you will be able to buy an AI from Dell for a few thousand dollars.

To be honest, I have to tell you that Kurzweil is one the most optimistic researchers. Almost everybody else believes that computers will need to perform ten to one hundred times more operations per second — one hundred million billion to one billion billion, or 10^{17} to 10^{18} — before being able to simulate a human brain. Nevertheless, with computing power growing exponentially, this would only add a delay of some years, not decades or centuries.[2]

Originally posted in my blog on 2010-07-21.

---

1 My predictions in the original article were somewhat optimistic. But On June 7th, 2014, the computer program called Eugene Goostman posing to be a 23-year-old Ukranian boy convinced 33% of the judges at the Royal Society in London that it was human (https://www.bbc.com/news/technology-27762088). Some AI experts have disputed the success of the test, but...

2 In the past few years, AI techniques and products have become almost commonplace in the form of Generative pre-trained transformers (GPT), which are large language models (LLMs) that generate text based on the semantic relationships between words in sentences. OpenAI release ChatGPT in 2022, but Google, Microsoft, Apple, and others have all been developing practical applications of LLMs.

The World as I see it

Of Soft Brains and Software Brains

An uninterrupted flood of information constantly bombards our senses: images, sounds, smells, tastes, textures, temperatures. We can cope with it because our brains only make us aware of a fraction of that information. We blissfully remain unaware of the rest.

This pruning of information is extremely efficient. Professor Thomas Landauer, while working at the Bell Laboratories, measured the amount of information that the human brain can handle in a second. It turns out that we can only memorise information at a maximum rate of 2 bits per second (2bps), which is very little. The Internet connection that most of us have at home can transfer data millions (Mbps) and billions (Gbps) times faster than that. We only manage to accumulate over the years so many memories because our brains don't actually save all the details all the times.

The brain records each event in a web of correlations and associations with other events. This way of storing information is very efficient but can become a source of frustration when we try to remember specific facts. We are sometimes unable to retrieve the piece of information we are looking for. And then, what finally pops into our conscious mind is a very subjective reconstruction of the original event.

To solve this problem, over the millennia, we have developed increasingly powerful methods for storing and retrieving information in more permanent and reliable ways. This path has taken us from painted rocks and clay tablets to modern computers.

Like with all other tools we have invented since the first chipped stone, computers provide an extension of our capabilities. They reliably store for us enormous amounts of data and operate on them at great speed. The question is whether we can make them think like us. Powerful enough hardware does not automatically result in an Artificial Intelligence. An AI also depends on the availability of especially designed software and efficient ways of interacting with the real world.

For longer than half a century AI researchers have been looking for ways of modelling a human-like intelligence with software. One of the hardest problems encountered has been the modelling of what we call common sense. For example, we wouldn't dream of picking up a fork to eat a soup. But a computer would need to be told that a spoon is what you use when you want to eat something liquid. We unconsciously use millions of such simple rules in our everyday activities. The task of capturing them all is (would be) enormous.

Fortunately, we don't need to endow a computer with the whole knowledge of humanity in order to make it intelligent. A bushman roaming the Kalahari desert is as intelligent as any other human being, despite the fact that he has probably never even seen most of the objects we use in our daily life. This type of considerations has motivated AI researchers to create what has become commonly known as expert systems (ES).

The purpose of an ES is to solve problems in a particular knowledge domain. By restricting the scope of the program, the researchers bring the amount of information down to manageable levels. All ESs work by asking questions until they can propose one or more possible solutions. They collect the symptoms of the problem, diagnose possible causes, and tell you what solutions are linked to the causes they have identified.

An ES bases its reasoning on a series of rules stored in its knowledge base. Each rule encodes an elementary step that a human expert would take when attempting to identify the problem. For example, a motor mechanic knows that an engine only starts if the battery is charged, the starter motor is in order, there is petrol in the tank, etc. Therefore, to determine why a particular car doesn't start, the mechanic checks the battery, listens to the starter motor, looks at the petrol gauge, etc. To make a motor mechanic ES, you would have to program into it a rule for each logical step the human expert would perform. For example, among many others, you would also include the rule that the engine only starts if the battery is charged. You would then need to link that rule to the description of how to check the status of the battery and what to do if the battery is flat.

In an ES, the whole problem-specific logic is stored in the rules, while the software is only an engine that, given the appropriate rules, could solve any problem. The key task of extracting knowledge from a human expert and formulate the corresponding ES rules is difficult because most experts are not aware of why they do what they do. The specialists who know how to tap into the mind of human experts are not programmers because they don't need to write any software. They call themselves knowledge engineers.

An ES can explain how it reaches its conclusions by listing all the rules its engine has encountered while solving the problem, and some ESs can provide several solutions, each with an associated probability. Several companies have developed commercial ESs, in particular to support medical practitioners in their diagnostic decisions[1]. These systems can be very useful, and more so in third world countries, where the number of doctors is very limited. Medical ESs can also help general practitioners with the correct diagnosis of seldom occurring diseases.

---

1 For example, MatheMEDics® (http://mathemedics.com/) develops and markets Web-based interactive medical decision support software for physicians, consumers and managed care providers.

To be able to provide more than one solution, the ESs need to cope with problems they don't have enough information to solve. This is not trivial because computers are based on binary logic. While we can weigh partially defined factors and arrive to conclusions that are reasonable or likely, computers only know yes and no. We use approximate values every day, but computers only accept precise inputs and provide precise answers. What makes the computers able to handle partially defined problems is a technique called fuzzy logic.

While standard logical variables can only be true or false, fuzzy variables can have several values. With fuzzy logic, values like *somewhat likely*, *fairly dark*, *quite heavy*, and *not too hot* are perfectly valid. You only need to define in advance what those fuzzy values mean in term of a continuous quantity. For example, somewhat likely might mean that you consider an event with a probability to occur between 51% and 60%. Similarly, not too hot might mean a temperature between 30 and 35 °C. With fuzzy logic a computer can handle cases in which value ranges overlap. A computer using crisp — as opposed to fuzzy — logic, in absence of a value like *somewhat likely*, would be forced to consider true an event with a probability of 51%. This might lead to confusing and/or inappropriate results.

While ESs manage to reproduce the thinking of human brains in restricted knowledge domains and handle partially defined problems with fuzzy logic, they will never be able to simulate a human mind in its entirety. This is because ESs are based on trees of logical choices codified in advance, while the neurons in our brain have a high level of connectivity that continuously evolves. The connections within and between areas of the brain are responsible for our intuition and hunches, on which innovation rests. To develop truly intelligent machines, we need to understand and reproduce the mechanisms of our mind, not just some of its results.

We have more or less one hundred billion neurons in our nervous system[1]. Each one of them can receive signals from up to ten thousand other neurons and send a signal to other neurons via a single output. When the sum of the signals received through its inputs exceeds a certain threshold, a neuron fires by doubling the electrical potential of its output (from 40-60 millivolts to 90-100 millivolts). The firing lasts about one millisecond, after which the neuron rests for at least 10 milliseconds before being ready to fire again.

At birth the neurons are only partially connected with each other. They can also form and modify connections easily. This explain for example why children can learn languages with much less effort than adults. As we grow up, more stable paths form within our brains, and our behavioural patterns become more difficult to change. Special neurons called mirror neurons seem to be very important for our learning processes. The special characteristic of these neurons is that they fire not only when we experience an emotion, but also when we see somebody else experiencing it. By doing so, they help us learn by imitation how to react to external events and how to behave in our community. They make us cry while we watch a dramatic or sentimental film because we experience through the mirror neurons the same feelings as the characters of the film. By simulating in our brain the actions of others, the mirror neurons also help us predict what the people we observe will do next.

Researchers have developed electronic circuits and software to simulate the workings of interconnected neurons. These Artificial Neural Networks (ANNs) are much more promising than ESs in the quest for true AI, but a lot of work still needs to be done. Like their natural counterparts, the artificial neurons accept a number of inputs and fire a single output.

---

1 Interestingly there are also 100 billion stars in our galaxy. A nice coincidence albeit without any meaning!

But, unlike what happens in the brain, the connections between neurons in an artificial networks remain unchanged after the initial setting[1]. What you can modify in ANNs is the way in which each neuron responds to its inputs and what level of signal it sends to its output.

What makes ANNs very useful for many applications — for example in computer vision — is their capability of learning. Optical Character Recognition (OCR) programs often use ANNs to identify printed and, somewhat less successfully, handwritten characters. These systems include at least three layers of artificial neurons. The first operation of such an OCR system is to scan the image of a character, break it down into a number of cells, and measure the darkness of each one of them. Figure 1 shows an example with the figure 9 scanned into 144 cells. The numbers in the top row show the levels of darkness of its cells, from 0 to 255 (which are the values you can store in an 8-bit byte of computer data).

Once completed the scan of a character, the OCR system passes the list of darkness values on to all neurons of the first ANN layer. Depending on their initial settings, some of the first layer neurons fire their outputs, which causes some of the neurons of the second layer to fire as well. The firing progresses through the layers until the neurons of the last layer fire. At this point, the OCR system uses the outputs of the last layer to reconstruct an image of the character and compares it with the initial scan, cell by cell. It then adjusts the settings of the output neurons to produce a better output. These corrections propagate back through the ANN causing an adjustment of all other neurons in the network, layer by layer. The OCR system repeats the whole procedure until the adjustments it has to make on the output neurons become

---

1 This is no longer true. Packages like ChatGPT "learn" the connections "learn" from huge amounts of data used to train them.

smaller than a predefined value. Through this training process, the ANN becomes able to recognise the scanned character. The things are in reality a bit more complicated because the system must be able to recognise many characters, not just one as in the example. But this should give you an idea of how the learning process work[1].

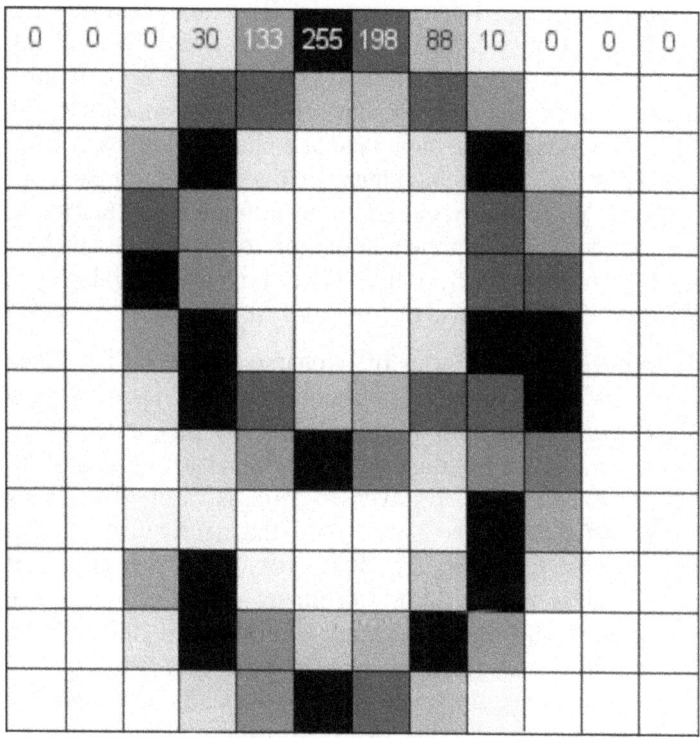

Figure 1: Sampling of an image for OCR

---

1 The same method, albeit more sophisticated, is used in fingerprint and face recognition, which for years has been routinely used around the world.

The World as I see it

The current research on computer vision focuses on recognising three-dimensional objects. It will still take a while before a computer will be able to distinguish between, say, an apple and a pear, but we are getting there[1]. This is essential research, if we want computers to be able to learn from their physical environment, as humans do in their childhood.

Despite the fact that our brains are the result of billions of years of natural evolution, it takes us several years to learn how to read and make sense of what we read. We keep learning for the entire duration of our lives and yet we only scratch the surface of what is there to be learned. This is because the total volume of knowledge of humanity is enormous and keeps expanding faster than any of us can hope to keep up with. But computers already store most of that knowledge and, within the next few decades, they will be able to begin understanding it. We will soon develop the software necessary for the computers to be able to continue their instruction on their own. When that will happen, they will no longer need us and, bit by bit (pun intended!), they might just decide to take charge. Today's computers are very dumb compared to us, but this shouldn't fool you into feeling safe in the supremacy of the human race.

Originally posted in my blog on 2010-07-21.

---

[1] I believe that in 2025 that is being routinely accomplished.

The World as I see it

AI Doesn't Really Think

This is a recent article that was never posted in my blog. After reading the previous articles, I feel that it is necessary to add something to cover the development in AI of the past fifteen years.

Why do I say that AI doesn't really think? If you have ever tried ChatGPT[1] you will know that its answers sound intelligent and well thought. It is actually amazing what you can get out of it!

But human thoughts are inestricably linked to life experiences and feelings, while those of AI are not. Our memories are spread over several areas of the brain, and the decisions we take depend of the associations we make and the trains of thought we follow. Although, to be truthful, the links that keep our memories together are weakened or reinforced with the passing of time, depending on our everyday experiences. Therefore, sometimes, we will not be able to explain all the decisions we take.

But AI bots do not make dynamic associations and do not even possess trains of thought to follow. Instead, they statically associate conceps because they happen to be close to each other in the texts the bots have been trained on. That is, they can only describe the what but never explain the why. If we get the feeling that AI bots can reason is because their textual databases include an ever-increasing amount of associations provided by humans.

The black-box architecture of AI bots means that the way in which they reach their conclusions is not just unknown or difficult to understand. It is unknowable![2] The only time we accept equally unexplainable statements made by human beings is when we are told that they were inspired by a God.

---
1 ChatGPT is a trade mark of OpenAI Global, LLC.

Indeed, the precipitous evolution of information technology has forced most of us into accepting the decisions made by computer software as an act of faith. How many times have you been told that "the computer says so" to shut you up? As if computers were infallible. AI is just a further step on the same path.

But AI bots *cannot even pretend to be truthful* because what they tell you is a combination of what human beings have stated, including racists, populist dictators, online influencers, spies with malicious intent, misogynists, bullies, fanatics of any type, etc.

The 'T' in GPT stands for transformer. And that's all AI chat bots do. They never create any new concept. They just collect facts and put them together because humans have put them beside one another in the past, perhaps in different contexts.

So, AI bots don't actually think.

In any case, most of what humans think never gets written down for AI bots to train on. For every article or story written, there are a miriad of thoughts that have not found their way to (so to speak!) paper.

I'm not against AI in general. Any profession that relies on analysing and maintaining vast amount of data can benefit from tailored AI applications, even if, in some cases, the applications might one day replace the human practitioners in professions like law and medicine, just to name two.

But we need to regulate the use of AI if we want to avoid abdicating parts of our humanity to it.

Donald Trump recently stated and insisted that in an American town some immigrants stole pet dogs and cats in

---

2 They are not Expert Systems, which can always explain the rules upon which they base their decisions.

order to eat them. The statement has been debunked but, with enough re-tweets, can you be sure that it will not be picked up by an AI bot?

Knowing how the online media actually encourage/prefer controversial statements in order to make more money regardless of whether the statements are true[1], the last thing you can do is accept a statement from an AI bot without independently verify it.

But how many people will do so considering that many believe that we never landed on the Moon? Two or three generations ago people sometimes said: "It must be true because I read it in the newspaper". The current generation easily believes what they read on social media. Soon, AI reports will become the repositories of truth. The problem is that there were handfuls of newspapers that checked on one another. But the millions and billions of social media users nowadays swallow whatever they like from their unchecked FaceBook, X, YouTube, and Istagram feeds. And AI bots can automatically generate trillions of fake news to serve any purpose without considerations of truthfulness.

To summarise, AI bots can only pair concepts that happen to be close to each other in the texts they can access; they don't create any new concept because they only use what is already there; they are biased towards what is trendy; and they don't have any concept of true or false.

Use at your own risk, and be aware that programs like ChatGPT are not free: you pay them with everything you type, which can (and will) then pop up on someone else's screen to use as if it were their own.

Originally written on 2024-09-22.

---

1 in 2025, Meta has removed fact checkers from FaceBook. Who cares whether a news is true if people like to click on it?

The World as I see it

From chipped stones to wearable computers

A couple of million years ago we learnt how to walk on our two hind limbs. Natural evolution selected it into our genes because it improved our chances of survival. We could see above the toll grasses of the Eastern African plains and detect approaching predators before it was too late. And once detected the danger, we could escape at a higher speed. But that evolutionary step also had another profound effect on our ancestors: it freed their hands. Some researchers actually believe that our ancestors started walking erect precisely to keep their hands free. This theory is somewhat controversial, but the end result is in any case the same.

Our cousins, the great apes, also use tools. Chimpanzees move objects to step on when they need to reach fruits hanging high above their heads. They also use sticks to collect termites and stones to crack nuts, but they cannot take their tools with them when they need to run. We could.

The initial tools we used strengthened and extended our arms. They were stones, sticks, and bones as we found them. We realised that certain shapes suited our purposes better than others, and started refining our tools. Thanks to the dexterity of our hands, we became a species of tool makers and inventors. Our motivation was survival, both as individuals and as a species. In that, we were exactly the same as any other animal, but we were unique in the way in which we went about it.

Instead of accepting the environment in which we lived, we did our best to modify it and insulate ourselves from natural dangers. We covered ourselves in clothes in order to survive in cold climates. We also learnt how to keep and create fire at will, so that we could chase away predators, stay warm in winter, and have light after sunset. Then, starting from around 10,000 BCE (Before Common Era) we tamed animals and seeded cereals, so that we could have a regular supply of food.

By 5,000 BCE farming was common in Asia and Europe. The planting of crops forced us to settle, and the first permanent villages came into existence. Supported by the increasing density of population in and around conglomerations, some people became specialist craftsmen and started producing goods for others. Trade thrived, and with it the need to measure and record properties and transactions. It led to the invention of writing, for which we have to thank the Sumerians.

They lived in Mesopotamia (a Greek word (Μεσοποταμία) that means 'between rivers'), the alluvial plain lying between the two rivers Tigris and Euphrates where parts of modern Iraq, Syria, and Turkye are. For some centuries, from around 3300 BCE, the Sumerians had made lists of valuable items by pressing little stamps on clay tablets and then baking them to preserve the imprints. But then, shortly after 3000 BCE, they started pressing on their tablets signs that corresponded to spoken sounds. For the first time, people were able to record and exchange any type of information. This marked the birth of History as we know it.

Writing made possible to transfer knowledge from place to place and from generation to generation in a reliable way. Thinkers and inventors could effectively build upon ideas and discoveries of others. During the following four and a half millennia, the medium used to write on changed from clay to papyrus, waxed tablets, parchment, and finally paper. But it was only with the invention of the printing press in mid fifteenth century that written information could reach everyone. Many more people could take advantage of the knowledge that already existed, and our intellectual and technological evolution took off.

In one way or another, most of the technological developments that have taken place during the past five and a half centuries have kept extending our senses and physical capabilities. With microphones, amplifiers, loudspeakers, earphones, radio, telephones, and mobile phones, we have become able to hear beyond the limits of our ears. With spectacles, telescopes, microscopes (optical, electronic, and tunnelling), night vision goggles, radar, radiography, magnetic resonance imaging (MRI), positron emission tomography (PET), and television, we have became able to see what our unaided eyes had not evolved to see. With bikes, trains, ships, submarines, lifts, motorcars, balloons, dirigibles, airplanes, parachutes, hang gliders, escalators, helicopters, and rockets, we have reached all corners of our world and beyond. With books, photography, magnetic tapes, vinyl records, cinematography, CDs, and DVDs, we have developed the means of saving the accumulated knowledge of billions of people.

Today, almost all the tools we use or know of are in fact extensions of ourselves, from the knife to the food processor, from the spade to the oil drill, from the hatchet to the nuclear bomb. During the second world war, we invented the digital computer. The first computers were bulky machines confined to climatised rooms and attended by technicians in white lab coats. Many thought that it would always be that way and that computers were so complicated that only professionally trained people could deal with them. But the introduction of transistors, with their reliability and small size, changed all that.

Around the mid 1960s the computers entered the normal office environment as minicomputers. For a while it seemed that the minis would be around forever, but their appeal already began to wane in the mid 1970s, when the first microprocessor-based systems hit the market. In 1977 Apple introduced the Apple II microcomputer, which became extremely popular in the education sector. Two years later, the Apple II broke into the business market with the introduction of the first spreadsheet software. It was only in the mid 1980s that macintoshes and personal computers began to replace the Apple II in homes and offices.

On October 29th, 1969, what was to become the Internet was born as a connection between UCLA (University of California Los Angeles) and SRI (Stanford Research Institute) International. By the late 1980s, the Internet connected almost 100,000 computers worldwide. They were mostly in universities and research institutions, although large and progressive companies had created their own private networks and exchanged data through the Internet via gateway systems[1]. The year 1990 saw the birth of the World Wide Web, through which personal computers have become our window to the world. Thanks to the Web, we can now tap sources of information and interact with each other in ways that were unthinkable just at the turn of the century.

For a couple of decades, computers remained for most of us something that we switched on and off when we needed them. Only during the past few years has the advent of fast wireless networks made access to the Internet almost ubiquitous[2].

The introduction of successive generations of mobile networks has blurred the distinction between telephones, computers, and television sets. With a handheld device you

---

1 You won't care, but I tell you anyway that in 1988, working for Prime R&D in Canberra, I was able to exchange emails with a friend of mine who was studying in San Diego.

2 Nowadays, more people use the Internet via smartphones than via laptops and desktops from home.

can now remain connected to the the rest of the world almost anywhere. And the current trend of using web services to store personal information (the Cloud) means that you are less and less bound to using the storage space provided by computers resting on or under your desk.

One of the limitations of modern handheld computers is the size of their screens. The Apple iPad and other tablet computers, with their 10-inch screens, are an exception, but they do not fit inside a shirt pocket. All major computer screen manufacturers like Fujitsu, Samsung, and Toshiba have been working on prototypes of flexible liquid crystal displays (LCD). But, although it will be nice to be able to take a large screen from a pocket and unfold it, I prefer the idea of using virtual screens.

A researcher who agrees with me is Steve Mann[1]. In 1970, while still in high school, he invented WearComp0, the first version of a wearable computer. His eye-tap captured the images seen by his right eye and sent them wirelessly to a remote computer for electronic analysis and manipulation. It then merged the result of the computer elaboration with the original images before presenting them to the eye.

Fighter jets use Head–Up Displays (HUD) to present information to the pilot via their helmet, but Steve Mann's eye-tap is much more than that because it transfers information in both directions. Steve describes it as mediated reality because his system can filter out and modify captured images, while HUDs can only superimpose data to what the pilot sees.

Today, Steve Mann is professor of Electrical and Computer Engineering at the University of Toronto. He has perfected his

---

1 https://www.eecg.utoronto.ca/~mann/ http://wearcam.org/ http://eyetap.org

invention to the level that it has become practically indistinguishable from a normal pair of sunglasses.

The latest versions of Prof. Mann's devices are so small and light that he can wear them for long periods of time. Life in such a video-mediated-reality develops its own thought processes. For example, he began pointing his finger at objects shown by the eye-tap but not present in the real world.

The wearable computer with an eye-tap opens up a host of new possibilities because it connects to other computers via wireless networks. For example, it makes possible to read emails via the eye-tap. Prof. Mann's group developed programs that analyse the mini-cam images and display emails only on suitable blank areas, like empty walls. Once attached to a wall present in the real world, the text of an email then moves in and out of sight together with it. It appears as if the email had been painted on the wall.

Prof. Mann built an eye-tap with a heat–sensitive camera. A remote computer connected to the eye-tap made the captured infrared images visible by associating different colours to different temperatures. This effectively provided night vision through eye-tap technology. In another test, Prof. Mann installed face recognition software on the remote computer. The eye-tap was then able to display the names of people that appeared in its field of vision.

Coupled with a GPS (Global Positioning System) device, the eye-tap can show route indications, both for walkers and for drivers.

Three technological developments have made possible for Prof. Mann to achieve such remarkable results: firstly, computers have become powerful enough to be able to process images in real time; secondly, wireless transmission has become fast enough to support the transfer of images forth and back without significant delay; and thirdly, the miniaturisation of electronic components has transformed the heavy backpacks of the first prototypes into light and unobtrusive devices.

Perhaps we will relate to wearable computers as we now relate to our clothes and the simple tools of everyday life, and they will become new status symbols. People will then show off their wearables as they now do with labelled clothing, watches and, increasingly, laptops and mobile phones. We will still take them off before going to bed or taking a shower, but wearables are only the next step on a path of increasing human–computer integration. I believe that many further steps will follow.

If you are concerned about the look of the eye-taps, don't be. Babak Parviz, an assistant professor of electrical engineering at the University of Washington, is working on contact lenses to replace external eye-taps. He unveiled the first prototype in January 2008. Although it was not functional, the prototype demonstrated that imaging and transmission circuitry could fit on a contact lens without impairing normal eyesight.

In any case, the main limitations of Prof. Mann's wearable computers are on the input side. Today you can only send commands to the computer via mini-keyboards. Voice input could improve the situation, but the privacy of the commands would normally be lost, as bystanders could hear them. The commands could be sub-vocalised and picked up by neck microphones, but it still doesn't seem the ideal solution.

What we should be able to do is to think our commands. We would formulate a query in our mind and see possible answers scroll directly before our eyes, or hear them whispered in our ear. This might seem far fetched, but it might only take less than a couple of decades before we will be able to do just that.

Originally posted in my blog on 2010-07-28.

The World as I see it

The World as I see it
Technology that gets under your skin

For the Merriam-Webster dictionary, Bionics is "a science concerned with the application of data about the functioning of biological systems to the solution of engineering problems". Similarly, Wikipedia defines Bionics as "the application of biological methods and systems found in nature to the study and design of engineering systems and modern technology". Bionics has many applications, but what interests me is that it helps develop devices that support, enhance, or even completely replace functions of the human body and, as such, they must become part of the people who carry them. They represent the first steps of man-machine integration.

Pirate and adventure films have made us all familiar with wooden pegs to replace severed legs and metal hooks replacing amputated hands. But prostheses have come a long way since those primitive devices. Modern artificial limbs, and in particular artificial hands, are very complex objects full of electronic circuitry. Sensors attached to the nervous system or the muscles of the amputee allow him to control the movements of a bionic limb. After a period of training, the movements of the artificial limb feel very similar to those of the natural limb before the amputation.

When you attempt to make a movement, the part of the brain in charge of movement control sends to the appropriate muscles electrical signals. These signals travel via nerves and cause on the skin surface weak but detectable voltage levels. Modern bionic limbs measure the voltages present on the skin to estimate strength and destination of the nerve signals. They then use that information to control mechanical actuators that emulate the muscles. This makes possible for an amputee to perform most of the operations he was able to do with his natural limb.

The World as I see it

The bones and tendons of mechanical limbs are made of steel and aluminium, and their muscles consist of electric actuators. This makes them potentially much stronger than their natural counterparts. It is therefore not surprising that some bioengineering companies have looked at ways of using the same technologies to strengthen able men. Perhaps the greatest advances in this area have taken place in Japan, which is a leader in the design and manufacturing of industrial robots.

For example, HAL 5, a robot suit[1] specifically designed to increase physical capabilities. It weighs approximately 23 kg and if it will probably be in full production when you read this essay. I have read that it could be yours to use for some fifteen thousand dollars plus a yearly maintenance fee.

Military organisations in most developed countries, and in particular the American Defense Advanced Research Projects Agency (DARPA), are very interested in this type of research. Already in the year 2000, the U.S. Army Natick Soldier Systems Center (NSSC) developed the Future Warrior Concept[2], which included the following central subsystems tailored to each individual:

- The Information Central, located in the headgear and providing maps, 180° display, very high speed broadband communication link, sensors covering 360°, and head protection.

- The Survivability Central, consisting of the following three layers of combat uniform: a protective outer layer

---

1 HALTM is a trade mark of Cyberdine Inc., and stands for Hybrid Assistive Limb. ROBOT SUIT® and CYBERDYNE® are registered trademarks of Cyberdine Inc.

2 This particular project was abandoned, but the military research to augment the capabilities of soldiers along similar lines is continuing.

made of electro-spun nanofibres, a power layer to augment the physical strength of the wearer, and the life critical inner layer. The life critical layer, directly in contact with the body of the wearer, is intended to have a monitoring function of vital signs, hydration state, stress level by means of mouth sensors, thermal state, sleep status, and workload capacity. Additionally, it includes a network of narrow tubing providing heating or cooling as needed. The life critical layer can also be used to administer nutrients, drugs, and other chemicals in response to injuries or other abnormal conditions.

- The Duration Central, consisting of a micro turbine generator. Each plug-in fuel cartridge can supply the necessary power for up to six days.

In future, soldiers on the battlefield will be nodes of a tactical network. They will be able to exploit the latest sensing and communication technologies to gain full awareness of their environment. A robotic suit will provide a protective exoskeleton while at the same time augmenting their physical capabilities. Robert Heinlein described something very similar in his novel *Starship Troopers*, published for the first time in 1959, but they will become reality in just a few years, well before humanity will reach the stars.

Robotic suits are exciting stuff, but other applications of bionics have proven themselves extremely useful for a wider part of humanity to overcome impairments. One example is the cochlear implant, often called bionic ear. Over the past forty years, more than one hundred thousand people worldwide have gained or regained their sense of hearing thanks to this device. It consists of two parts, one surgically implanted on the side of the head, and one external. The two parts communicate through skin and muscle via radio waves.

The implanted part consists of a thin electrode that coils inside the snailshell-like cochlea and a thicker part housing the radio antenna and electronic circuitry. The external part consists of a headpiece with the antenna, a microphone, and a sound processor.

Normally, hearing cells stimulate the auditory nerve in response to mechanical stimuli from the inner ear. When these cells are unable to perform their function, the result is one form of complete deafness. The bionic ear resolves the problem by capturing sounds with the microphone, converting them to the appropriate electrical signals with the sound processor, and directly stimulating the auditory nerve with its thin electrode.

Hip and in general joint replacements are other applications of bionics that have become commonplace. Although they require more invasive surgery than bionic ears, such operations are conceptually simpler, and a well established industry has developed around them. The same is true for artificial heart valves. But the replacement of a whole heart with an artificial one is another matter.

Over the past decades, heart transplants have almost become routine. More than two thirds of the patients live longer than five years after the operation, and some conduct a normal life for decades. But all around the world the number of people in desperate need of heart replacement significantly exceeds the number of donors. Moreover, transplant recipients are forced to take anti-rejection medication for the rest of their lives. As immune rejection is caused by differences between the genetic make-ups of donor and recipient, an artificial heart causes milder reactions.

With the current level of technology and medical care, an artificial heart can extend the life of the recipient by longer than one year. Although this is not enough to make artificial hearts suitable as permanent replacements, it is often sufficient to keep the patients alive until a donated heart becomes available. One of the most successful artificial hearts to date is the Jarvik-7 heart, implanted in hundreds of patients since 1982[1].

In any case, while natural organs continuously regenerate and repair themselves and can therefore last for decades, the mechanical components of their artificial counterparts are subject to wear and fail after maximum a few years of operation. The biotechnologists need to overcome this obstacle if artificial hearts are to become truly permanent.

There are many other prostheses in different stages of development. For example, retinal implants aim at restoring eyesight by converting light to electrical impulses and then directly stimulating the optical nerves. This follows the successful strategy adopted for the bionic ear and has had some limited success.

All the examples I have presented so far consist of self-contained electromechanical devices to replace or complement the functioning of limbs and organs. But several researchers are concentrating their efforts in a different direction. They use active electronic circuits to stimulate or suppress individual functions of our organs. The most widely known example of these applications is the heart pacemaker.

The human heart, like the heart of all mammals, consists of two pairs of chambers. The pair on the right side pumps blood

---

[1] https://www.jarvikheart.com/ But the Jarvik-7 heart does not replace the original heart. Instead, it supports it and assists it. The Carmat artificial heart, a fully functional mechanism to replace the biological heart, was approved for sale in the EU, receiving a CE marking on 22 December 2020. As of December 2023, the Carmat is available in Europe as a bridge-to-transplant, for up to 180 days while awaiting a human heart transplant.

to the lungs where it can absorb oxygen. The pair on the left side pumps blood through the whole body so that it can deliver its oxygen to where it is needed. Each pair consists of two chambers connected via a unidirectional valve, similar to the valves found in bicycle pumps. When the first chambers of the pairs (each called atrium, a Latin word that means courtyard) simultaneously contract, the blood they contain is pushed through the valves to the corresponding second chambers (each called ventricle, from a Latin word that means small belly). A tenth of a second later, a second contraction squeezes the ventricles and pushes the blood out of the heart.

This pumping cycle, our heart beat, repeats on average eighty times a minute. Each cycle starts when a group of nerve cells located in the right atrium (called sinus node) causes the heart to contract by stimulating it with electrical impulses. When the sinus node doesn't work properly or when the electrical impulses it generates fail to reach their destination, it becomes necessary to stimulate the heart with an artificial pacemaker.

Modern pacemakers can control the whole heart and sense changes in the movement and respiration of the carrier to adjust the pulse rate accordingly. Furthermore, they only activate when they detect that the heart needs pacing, thereby extending their operational life to ten or more years.

The new frontier of implants is in deep brain stimulation (DBS). As scientists gain a better understanding of how the brain works, new techniques become available to control the effects of brain damage and brain diseases. DPS makes possible for people with Tourette syndrome and Parkinson to conduct an almost normal life. The epileptic crisis suppressor works along similar lines but operates on different parts of the brain. How long before you will be able to buy a device to stimulate the pleasure centres of your brain?

Originally posted in my blog on 2010-07-31.

MANAGEMENT

Management - Trust

The word trust is for company life what love is for the movie industry: so much used and so often abused that most people develop for it the same self-protecting indifference that nurses and doctors must have for blood.

I checked out three different dictionaries, one Australian (The Macquarie Dictionary), one English (Collins Dictionary of the English Language), and one American (The American Heritage Dictionary of the English Language). Their first definitions of trust sound as follows: "Reliance on the integrity, justice, etc., of a person, or on some quality or attribute of a thing, confidence"; "Reliance on and confidence in the truth, worth, reliability, etc., of a person or thing; faith"; "Firm reliance; confident belief; faith".

The only two words all those definitions have in common are *reliance* and *faith*. But then, how do you reconcile the trust that many managers claim to have in their employees with their obsessive checking, reviewing, verifying, controlling? The answer is very simple: you cannot. To put it bluntly with a nice cliché: you can't have the cake and eat it too! The more closely you need to check on what somebody does, the less you can claim to trust her integrity, quality, and reliability.

Some years ago, I worked for the Swiss subsidiary of a large telecommunication company. Engineers still had to stamp cards four times a day to record their working hours, and managers were supposed to check the cards and sign them for approval at the end of each month. As soon as I took over the responsibility of a software development department, I called everybody in and told them: "As you know, I am responsible for ensuring that your stamp-cards are correctly filled in before passing them on to administration. I find this equivalent to treating you like children, rather than responsible professionals. Therefore, I shall not check any card. At the end of each month, I will just see that you have filled them in, sign them up, and pass them on. Please don't put me in a difficult situation with the bean counters. Further, if you want to take half a day or one full day off work, please do not ask me. Let me know before you go, but don't wait for my approval because you are not going to get any. A note on my desk or an email will do. You are the best person to know whether you can take time off without compromising the project you are working on. Who am I to decide the importance of what you have to do at home? Aren't we supposed to be responsible adults?"

I was strongly criticised by *my* superior for taking such a stand but, ultimately, how and whether I checked on my people was my call.

In two occasions the administration detected mistakes in one of the cards and sent it back to me, but that was a small price to pay for showing to my engineers that I trusted them. The guy whose card was sent back (the same person in both occasions) felt that he had let me down and was very sorry to have caused me problems. I like to think that he didn't do it with malicious intent.

I was the first manager in a company of almost two thousand people to challenge that regulation. The stamp-cards were abolished a couple of years later, totally independently of my stand, but I could have not waited for it to happen. For me, it was a matter of principle.

Anyhow, the engineers were so used to being kept on a short leash that some found it difficult to adjust to the newly gained freedom. In several occasions, people came to me and asked me whether I thought they could take the next day off. "You just want to shy away from your responsibility", I always replied. "If you have to ask me whether you can stay at home, it probably means that you shouldn't, and you know it. I am definitely not going to leave you off the hook. Freedom always comes with responsibility and this is entirely your call". You should have seen their faces... They had to grow up and couldn't go anymore to 'daddy' and ask for a favour!

After a while, everybody got accustomed to working that way and took it for granted that it wasn't the boss's task to check on people's presence in the office.

Obviously, if I had been inconsistent with my statements and checked the cards, I would have lost all credibility and, with it, the trust of my people. And this brings me to a crucial question concerning reciprocal trust: can an untrusting person be trustworthy? I would tend to answer no. People often project onto others what they think or feel true for themselves. This is cheap psychology, but you know that I am right. Then, what does this tell you about a boss who is concerned that you overload your expense claims or spend too much time at the coffee machine?

Originally posted in my blog on 2010-07-13.

Management - Decisions

A leader should decide as little as possible.

Many people find it difficult to decide. They agonise on alternatives and keep postponing the moment when they finally must commit themselves to one of them. When I say that a leader should decide as little as possible I certainly don't mean that.

There is a big difference between not being able to do something and deciding not to do it. What I mean with deciding as little as possible is that a leader should leave as much decisional space as possible to the people reporting to her. Only in that way can she empower her collaborators and add meaning to their jobs.

Let me give you a real-life example. In one occasion, I had a group of twelve engineers working on a critical project. We had agreed on tasks and schedule, but it wasn't yet completely clear who would do what. Most managers would have simply assigned the tasks in what they believed to be the best possible way, perhaps after some consultation with the most senior engineers. I took a different approach: I called the whole team into a meeting room and announced that they would decide the task assignments themselves. Before leaving them alone, I said: "I don't really care how long it will take, but I expect that you will not leave this room without a name beside each task."

It was a very successful operation, and the commitment of each one of them received a great boost. It is mostly arrogance from the part of the managers that makes them believe to know more about everybody's skills. The team members know perfectly well what they and their colleagues can (or cannot) do.

In general, the idea that a manager is paid to make decisions is a bad misconception. A manager is mainly paid to achieve results through her collaborators. "Who decides what" is totally irrelevant.

This doesn't mean that a manager never has to decide anything. In fact, any manager has to make decisions every day. The issue really is: who decides by default. In my opinion, instead of asking herself whether she could delegate a decision to her collaborators, a manager should ask: "Do I really need to take this decision away from them?"

In most cases, the decisions are pretty straightforward, but the attitude I just described is necessary to actually implement what is nowadays called employee empowerment.

Like in everything involving human beings, the major risk is to go overboard and come across as a manager who is not capable of deciding. Two major aspects must be kept in mind:

1. It must be clear that the manager always has overrule and veto rights.
2. Enough information must be available for the team member[s] to decide.

Originally posted in my blog on 2010-07-14.

Management - Where the Buck Stops

I have always entertained very informal relationships with my collaborators and allowed them to decide in as many situations as feasible. This was only possible because, besides being friendly and open, I systematically made clear that I had the overall responsibility and that, therefore, could overturn any decision made by a team member.

It is very easy for people to confuse a team led by a friendly boss with a democratic group of equals. This is never the case and you must make it very clear. A company is at best a constitutional monarchy, rather than a democracy.

The only way for the system I am advocating to work is to draw clear lines and delimit responsibilities. In doubt, a collaborator is forced to ask her boss for confirmation, and that is equivalent to passing up the responsibility for a decision.

There will always be misunderstandings, and even people in bad faith that abuse their bosses' tolerance. Nevertheless, it is extremely important to set clear limits to what everybody can decide upon.

For example, in a software development group, it is essential for each engineer to know the scope of her work. It is also essential for her to be able to work within those limits without external interference.

That's why engineers who accept promotions to management positions only because of prestige or money usually become bad leaders: they cannot leave the fingers off the tasks that no longer belong to them.

An example: an engineer has been wrestling with a complex algorithm for a couple of days. Clearly, she needs more support than she is getting. The manager could sit together with her and inject some order into her thoughts, perhaps suggest some steps to implement intermediate algorithms before tackling the final one. But when the manager is asked for support, instead of advising the engineer on how to proceed, she sits down, codes 80% of the algorithm, and passes it on to the engineer to figure out the last details.

Does it sound familiar? How does that make the engineer feel? What does it do to her self-esteem?

The next time, that engineer is likely to give up much more easily and turn directly to the boss. Incidentally, this is why so many development project managers are horribly overworked: beside their own jobs, they also have to do the jobs of their collaborators.

True, sometimes there are no alternatives for a manager to stepping in and taking charge of a blocked situation, but such an action should only represent a last resort, when everything else has failed.

Like in everything else, there is no simple rule for finding the right balance between controlling and letting go. Inexperienced team members must be supervised more closely, and new hires must be taken by hand for a while, regardless of how much experience they have accumulated before joining your team.

Perhaps the single most important thing that a manager can do is to be aware of these issues, express them clearly to her collaborators, and admit her mistakes openly.

Originally posted in my blog on 2010-07-14.

Management - Need to Know

How can people decide with competence if they don't have all the information they need in order to do it? In one respect, human beings are like any other machine: to deliver good results they need to have the necessary inputs and be able to process them well enough.

Let's face it, there are capable people and less capable ones. To pretend that all team members are equal and should be treated in the same way is ridiculous. For certain activities, the level of productivity of the team members can differ from one another by a factor of ten or more. One well known example of this variability is the number of tested and delivered lines of code written in a third generation programming language like C or Java.

This means that a manager cannot have the same expectations regarding all her team members.

This also means that some team members need more from their manager than others. If I can make an unorthodox parallel, some collaborators are like delivery trucks, slow, reliable, and supporting heavy loads; others are like racing cars, temperamental, quick, and extremely performing; some others are like a combination of the two, perhaps with elements of mini-buses or medium-sized family cars.

Now, for team work to succeed, you need all sorts of team members, and it is your task as a leader to recognise their differences, utilise their qualities at best, and provide to them whatever they need to function.

Most importantly, everybody must have access to information, both directly related to their job and to the company in general. Withhold information from your team and you will seriously impair their ability to decide autonomously. This is perfectly consistent with the concept that knowledge is power: keep your people in the dark and all your talks of empowerment become lip service.

In fact, this is precisely why so many managers do not inform their collaborators: to prevent them from making decisions and be in the loop in as many decisions as possible. These are the control freaks who want to know everything but only dispense information allegedly on a need-to-know basis. In reality, they apply the old Roman strategy of the *divide et impera* (divide and rule), creating little privileges for individual team members and thereby completely undermining team building.

Bottom line? Apply to the distribution of knowledge a criterion equivalent to what I recommended for making decisions: say everything by default. That is, ask yourself whether there are reasons for withholding information rather than reasons for passing it on. Further, create automatisms to distribute information, so that you must consciously decide to stop a news item to be distributed, while everything is forwarded to others by default.

Originally posted in my blog on 2010-07-14.

Management - Guidelines vs Rules

A lot of people think that guidelines, leaving some leeway and ambiguity, are less restrictive than fixed rules. This is certainly not the case, at least not in general. To convince yourself, try to answer this question: "Who decides whether an action conforms to a guideline or not?"

Perhaps you already see where I am getting to: a guideline leaves space for different interpretations, but which interpretation is right depends on the inclination or even the mood of a manager. That's why a manager who formulates more guidelines than regulations can well be the worst control freak there is.

Let me give you a real-life example: travel expenses. The document that tells you what you can and cannot claim states that the company will not reimburse you for what you take from the minibar of your hotel room. Well, we all know that drinks from the minibar are very expensive. Moreover, why should the company pay for your booze? Still, you arrive late in the evening after a full working day and hours spent in airports, airplanes, and taxis; shouldn't you be able to take a mineral water (or, God forbid, even a beer!) from the minibar on company expenses? I certainly think so.

Now, let's see the implication of having guidelines or regulations. If the no-minibar is a rule, people can, with reason, air vocal complaints. If, on the other hand, it is only a guideline, the manager can say: "Don't worry, nobody is going to make you pay for your mineral water. These are just guidelines and will be applied with flexibility and reason". What can you answer to that? In practice though, it means that the manager (or even, in some cases more realistically, the secretary) approving your expense claims will be able to use her discretion, thereby depriving you of your decisional power.

One possible way out of this is to say that expense claims do not need managerial approval. To avoid possible abuses (there can always be rotten apples in any crate), the claims could be checked anonymously. Systematic deviations would then lead to further investigations and a tightening up of the process. Such a system seems complicated but it isn't: first of all, the check could be done by any support staff with limited qualifications. Secondly, it would give freedom to the employees as long as they do not systematically abuse the regulations.

For example, suppose that a per diem of $100 is budgeted for meals. As long as the average daily amount spent on meals calculated across all expense claims remains below that figure, does it really matters than during a trip some might have spent 150 dollars in some occasions and only $50 in others?

In general, a good strategy for avoiding unfairness is to reduce the level of details of the regulations. For example, why should you set separate limits for breakfast, lunch, and dinner, rather than a single daily limit for meals? Besides making the checks more time consuming, it significantly reduces the flexibility of the traveller.

So, am I suggesting that we should only have fixed rules with inflexible limits? Not at all. The purpose of this section is only to show you how apparently enlightened managers can in fact leave less freedom than less flexible ones.

A possible alternative solution is to have guidelines but not leave exclusively to the manager the task of checking whether they are correctly applied or not. Suppose for example that, whenever a manager objects to an expense, a group of employees decides whether the expense should be refunded or not. It would be a real pain to do, but would quickly result in a list of applicable guidelines and, after a dozen trips, discussions would no longer be necessary. Obviously, as a manager, you can only apply such a method if you have established a relationship of trust with your team. Otherwise, you might discover that they always approve every claim...

Another possible solution would be to have employees check the expense claims of the manager. You can rest assured that most managers would find themselves in very tight situations. This is, in a different context, equivalent to peer or 360-degree reviews.

The bottom line on this subject is, once more, use common sense.

Originally posted in my blog on 2010-07-15.

The World as I see it

Management - Generosity

Keep the others indebted to you.

What do I mean by that? It is simple, really: as long as your collaborators will feel that they owe you something or, better said, as long as they don't feel squeezed dry by you, they will bend over backward with their work to make you happy.

If you are generous with your collaborators, when the need arises, you can also ask special efforts from them and expect that they will do their best to satisfy your requests. If you, on the other hand, never give away anything without first cashing in, you will find it very difficult to ask for more in emergencies.

This is of course not independent of trust, as you cannot possibly give if you expect people to be selfish and uncommitted.

Obviously, the risk exists that people will exploit your trust, take advantage of your generosity, and laugh behind your back. Nevertheless, you cannot really achieve anything without risking something. There is a scene of an interesting piece of theatre that illustrates this situation. I think it is from the Italian author and actor Eduardo De Filippo. It goes like this: Every morning, a man crumbles a piece of bread on the window sill and rejoices at the sight of pigeons pecking on the crumbs. "They must be very grateful", he reflects. The pigeons, on the other hand, while gorging themselves on the bread, think: "How silly this old man. We steal his bread every day and he keeps putting it out."

Many managers are afraid to be seen as the man of that scene is seens by the pigeons. I had a manager who, no matter what I told him, before trying to understand what I meant, seemed to be asking himself: "Why is he saying that? What is his hidden agenda? What is he REALLY trying to achieve with his words?" Not much trust there!

I will be honest with you: There WILL be people who will take advantage of your generosity, but many more who will value it and respect you more for it. Ultimately, I don't really care whether somebody thinks about me like the pigeons about the man in the story. I am confident that, over the months, I will be able to recognise the bad apples and weed them out.

It is only when you give that you can then expect to receive. To give you a practical example, how can you refuse to stay till late to solve a problem if your boss always lets you organise your working day as you like? It would really be petty of you to refuse to come on a Saturday for an emergency if you were always able to be at home for your family's events. Don't you think?

Another example. Who has never taken home from work some stationery, or even just a pencil, should raise her hand. Let's face it, we all do it. How much does this cost to the company? Ten dollars per year per employee? One hundred? Is it really worth arguing about it? And what about free coffee and drinks? And yet, how would an employee feel if she had to ask the departmental secretary when she needs a new note pad? I tell you, it pays to be generous. Often, the small things are those which create a positive atmosphere in the workplace and contribute to staff retention.

Originally posted in my blog on 2010-07-17.

Management - My Leadership Principles

In no particular order and with plenty of redundancy!

1. Any goal is impossible until you find the way to achieve it.
2. You only fail when you give up trying.
3. You cannot be the best unless you learn how to improve.
4. You cannot win unless you bet.
5. Take one step at a time but don't ever stop.
6. Your success depends more on what you believe than on what is true.
7. Ask yourself whether you deserve what you are getting before trying to get what you think you deserve.
8. The only real proof that you can do something is that you have already done it.
9. The tiniest lie has the power of compromising the greatest truth.
10. No lie is small enough to be insignificant.
11. The less you say, the more you will be listened to.
12. From the back you can only push. Get in front if you want to lead.
13. One picture counts more than thousand words, but a few good words can count more than thousand bad pictures.
14. Listen to your emotions but don't let them take over.
15. It is better to show emotions than to be an emotional cripple.

The World as I see it

16. Unexpressed ideas don't count.
17. It's easy to reach an agreement with those who already think like you.
18. It's easy to bring good news.
19. The worst jails are those we create ourselves.
20. The highest the pedestal you put yourself on, the less you will hear the people around you.
21. It's easy to delegate what you don't like to do.
22. If you open trapdoors before people, watch your own steps.
23. You can only claim that you trust somebody if you don't check on him.
24. It's difficult to get anywhere if you keep your eyes shut.
25. You cannot be a leader without taking sides.
26. Before making any decision, ask yourself whether somebody else could do it. If yes, let him.
27. If you must decide, do it now.
28. You must admit your mistakes if you want to learn from them.
29. There cannot be improvement without expressing negative opinions.
30. Don't hesitate in criticising what people do but never criticise people for what they do.
31. It's easier to find faults than to see what is missing.
32. You can only see further if you stick your neck out.
33. Listen to those who stay quiet and talk to those who speak a lot.

34. You don't always need to say something in order to tell people off.

35. Don't hope to be trusted if you cannot trust.

36. Don't offend the intelligence of people by telling them what they know that you are not thinking.

37. To delegate a decision after telling what you would do is no delegation at all.

38. If you treat adults like children, don't be surprised when they put up a tantrum.

39. An undeserved praise can be more damaging than an unjustified reproach.

40. You seldom get more than what you ask for.

41. Give before you ask.

42. The more you try to make people lose, the less likely you will win.

43. If you win, be generous with the losers.

44. Try to be as successful as others, rather than attempting to make them as unsuccessful as yourself.

45. If you don't know where you are going, don't expect to get there soon.

46. Improvements are changes and there are no changes without risks.

47. If you are not sure whether to say something, why should you decide not to?

48. Silences are more often misunderstood than words.

49. If you cannot express something in few words, then use many.

The World as I see it

50. If you cannot make small changes, don't expect to be able to make big ones.

51. Any destination is unreachable if you don't know where you are.

52. Every thousand mile journey begins with a single step (Ghandi).

53. Before you accepts something free of charge, be sure that you can afford it.

54. What is the point of telling lies to somebody who doesn't believe what you say?

55. The less you need something, the more people will be willing to give it to you.

56. Don't confuse being innocent with not having been caught.

57. Perhaps you cannot always say what you think, but at least don't say what you don't think.

58. Don't confuse politeness with friendliness.

59. You cannot convince who doesn't want to be convinced.

60. To be generous with what doesn't matter is cheap.

61. Don't try to explain the unexplainable.

62. You don't always need to control your emotions, but never let them control you.

Originally posted in my blog on 2010-07-18 and 2010-07-19.

The World as I see it

Appendix

The Italian original of the email I sent to leave the Catholic Church.

Subject: Istanza ai sensi dell'art. 7 del Decreto Legislativo n. 196/2003.

From: Giulio Zambon

Date: Tue, 03 Nov 2009 15:13:29 +1100

To: sangiuseppe-crl@libero.it

Al Parroco della parrocchia San Giuseppe a Via Nomentana

Via Francesco Redi 1

00161 Roma

Io sottoscritto Giulio Zambon, nato a Roma, il [birth date removed], *residente a Harrison (Australia) e iscritto all'Albo dei cittadini Italiani Residenti all'Estero (AIRE) di Roma, con la presente istanza, presentata ai sensi dell'art. 7, comma 3, del Decreto Legislativo n. 196/2003, mi rivolgo a Lei in quanto responsabile dei registri parrocchiali.*

Essendo stato sottoposto a battesimo nella Sua parrocchia, in una data a me non nota ma di poco successiva alla mia nascita, desidero che venga rettificato il dato in Suo possesso, tramite annotazione sul registro dei battezzati, riconoscendo la mia inequivocabile volontà di non essere più considerato aderente alla confessione religiosa denominata "Chiesa cattolica apostolica romana".

Chiedo inoltre che dell'avvenuta annotazione mi sia data conferma sia per posta elettronica che per lettera, debitamente sottoscritta e indirizzata a Giulio Zambon [my sister's address in Italy removed]

Si segnala che, in caso di mancato o inidoneo riscontro alla presente richiesta entro 15 giorni, mi riservo, ai sensi dell'art. 145 del Decreto Legislativo n. 196/2003, di rivolgermi all'autorità giudiziaria o di presentare ricorso al Garante per la protezione dei dati personali.

Dichiaro di rinunciare fin da subito a qualsivoglia pausa di riflessione o di ripensamento in ordine alla soprascritta istanza; avverto che considererò ogni dilazione come rifiuto di provvedere nel termine di legge (15 giorni, ai sensi dell'art. 146, comma 2, del D. lgsn. n. 196/2003) e che quindi intendo immediatamente ricorrere all'autorità giudiziaria o al Garante per la tutela dei dati personali, qualora Lei illegittimamente differisse l'annotazione richiesta ad un momento successivo al quindicesimo giorno dal ricevimento della presente.

Ciò, in ottemperanza del Decreto Legislativo n. 196/2003 (che ha sostituito, a decorrere dall'1/1/2004, la previgente Legge n. 675/1996), in ossequio al pronunciamento del Garante per la protezione dei dati personali del 13/9/1999 ed alla sentenza del Tribunale di Padova depositata il 29/5/2000.

Si diffida dal comunicare il contenuto della presente richiesta a soggetti terzi che siano estranei al trattamento, e si avverte che la diffusione o la comunicazione a terzi di dati sensibili può configurare un illecito penale ai sensi dell'art. 167 del D.lgs. n. 196 del 2003.

Si allega fotocopia del passaporto quale documento d'identità.

Distintamente, Giulio Zambon

www.ingramcontent.com/pod-product-compliance
Lightning Source LLC
Chambersburg PA
CBHW020748160426
43192CB00006B/277